HARNESSING THE SUN

DAVID C. KNIGHT

HARNESSING
THE SUN

THE STORY
OF SOLAR ENERGY

illustrated with photographs and diagrams
William Morrow and Company
New York   1976

opposite: Portion of the huge parabolic mirror at the solar furnace system in Font-Romeu, France.
Centre National de la Recherche Scientifique

Library of Congress Cataloging in Publication Data

Knight, David C.
  Harnessing the sun.

  SUMMARY: Discusses the energy given off by the sun and its past, present, and potential usefulness to man.
  1. Solar energy—Juvenile literature. [1. Solar energy] I. Title.
TJ810.K55   333.7   75-44301
ISBN 0-688-22070-3
ISBN 0-688-32070-8 lib. bdg.

BY THE SAME AUTHOR
Eavesdropping on Space
Thirty-Two Moons
The Tiny Planets

The author wishes to express his thanks and appreciation to Dr. Lloyd Motz, of Columbia University, for checking his manuscript.

CONTENTS

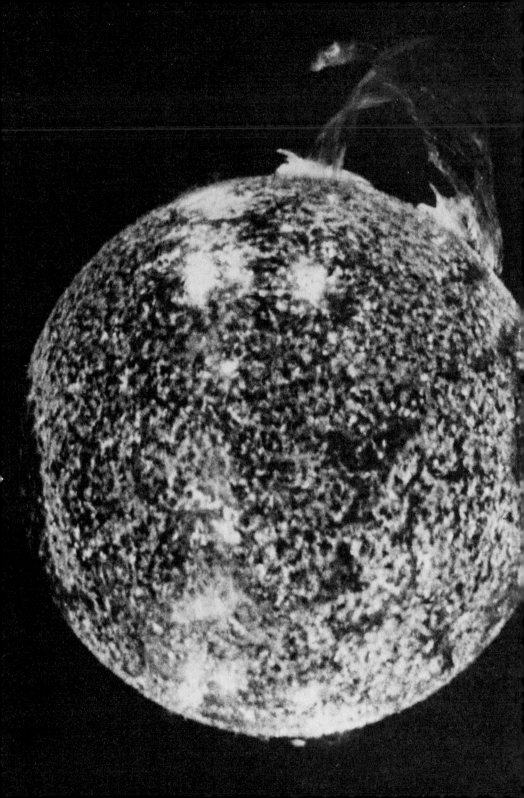

CHAPTER ONE

MEET THE SUN

Our star the sun, into which could fit one million planets the size of the earth, sends out, or emits, incredibly vast amounts of energy. This energy is called "solar" energy, from the Latin word *sol,* meaning sun. The flow of solar energy from the sun never stops; nor will it ever stop until our star reaches the end of its life billions of years from now.

It is difficult to imagine the enormous quantity of energy constantly emanating from the sun. Suppose that instead of water gasoline flowed over Niagara Falls at the same rate— 5 billion gallons per hour. Now suppose that all the gasoline that passed over the Falls for more than 200 million years could be collected. If all that gasoline were burned, it would about equal the energy that the sun emits in one single hour.

What processes are going on inside the sun to produce such a limitless supply of energy? Solar energy is the end result of nuclear reactions constantly taking place in the sun's

opposite: This photograph of the sun, taken by the crew of Skylab 4, shows one of the most spectacular solar flares ever recorded, spanning more than 367,000 miles across the solar surface. *NASA*

interior. These reactions involve the nuclei, or central parts, of atoms. In a nuclear reaction, a small amount of matter can be transformed into a large amount of energy. Because the sun contains such vast amounts of matter, continually undergoing nuclear change, it can emit this colossal flow of energy.

During these reactions, the sun changes hydrogen atoms into helium atoms at the incredible temperature of 27 million degrees Fahrenheit. Every second our star converts 564.5 million tons of hydrogen into 560 million tons of helium. What happens to the missing 4.5 million tons of matter that did not become helium? It is emitted in all directions into space as pure radiant, or solar, energy. Fortunately, only about two billionths of it reaches the earth, and a fraction of that reaches our sensitive skins; if much more reached us, our planet would be unlivable for obvious reasons.

The rest of this solar energy is radiated into empty space. The small part that strikes the earth, after traveling ninety-three million miles from its source, is further reduced by reflection from the atmosphere and absorption by the ozone layer high in the earth's atmosphere. Scientists have calculated that the sun, at the start of its life as a luminous star, began to give off this nuclear energy some five billion years ago. They believe that it will continue to radiate this energy for about another ten billion years.

Two terms—*energy* and *power*—are used to describe the sun's radiation and how it is measured. Sometimes these

terms are confused. The sun produces energy—solar energy
—not power; solar energy is what reaches the earth, not
solar power. Power is the *rate* at which solar energy is produced. Scientists and engineers use a unit called a "kilowatt"
(1000 watts) to measure power. But to measure energy—in
this case, solar energy—the unit normally used is the kilowatt
hour; that is, the energy expended by one kilowatt in one
hour at the rate of one kilowatt.

The sun continuously produces an estimated 390 sextillion
(390 followed by 21 zeros) kilowatt hours of energy. But
the sun gives off its energy in all directions, because it is a
spherical body. This is the reason why the upper atmosphere
of the earth receives only a small fraction of the sun's total
energy output.

Even so the earth receives more than 1500 quadrillion
(1500 followed by 15 zeros) kilowatt hours of energy from
the sun each year. Imagine a coal train long enough to reach
from the earth to the moon and back five times. If all the
coal on this train were burned, it would produce the same
amount of energy that the earth's upper atmosphere receives
from the sun in one hour. Actually, several different types
of radiant energy from the sun strike the atmosphere. The
most important ones are light, infrared (heat), radio, ultraviolet, and X rays.

Scientists also have a term for the average amount of solar
energy normally received at the outer layer of the earth's

9

atmosphere. It is called the "solar constant" and amounts to nearly two calories per square centimeter per minute. (A calorie is the amount of heat required at sea level to raise the temperature of one gram of water one degree centigrade.) This would mean that a square yard of the outer layer of the earth's atmosphere continuously receives per second an amount of solar energy equivalent to nearly two horsepower. (One horsepower is roughly equivalent to the average rate at which a horse can work; as a unit of power, it is 550 foot-pounds per second.) Sometimes the solar constant is expressed in langleys, in honor of the American astronomer Samuel Pierpont Langley, who also did pioneer work in practical applications of solar energy. The langley is defined as a unit of solar radiation equivalent to one gram calorie per square centimeter of surface upon which sunlight falls.

Not all the solar energy that arrives from the sun manages to penetrate to the surface. Figures vary, but about 34 percent is scattered into space by the gases and dust in the atmosphere or is directly reflected back into space by clouds. About 19 percent is absorbed by the different layers of the atmosphere. The remaining 47 percent finally reaches the ground or oceans, where it is absorbed as heat.

Scientists estimate that more than 700 quadrillion kilowatts of solar power reach the earth's surface each year. Yet man uses only about 50 trillion kilowatts of power to run all of his factories, machines, and vehicles and to heat all of his buildings. Thus, in about forty minutes the sun delivers to the earth's surface as much energy as mankind uses in a year's time. One scientist has calculated that the amount of solar energy that falls on the United States alone in one minute is enough to supply the total energy needs of the whole country for one day. Such comparisons clearly show how gigantic an amount of potential power is lost to man every hour, every day, and every year.

With all this boundless energy constantly bombarding the earth, what are its effects on our planet? First and foremost, without the warmth provided by solar radiation, the earth would be a barren, frozen place, devoid of life.

Solar energy is also the main cause of the weather changes

Diagram showing how the atmosphere affects the amount of solar energy reaching the earth. Percentages are approximate.

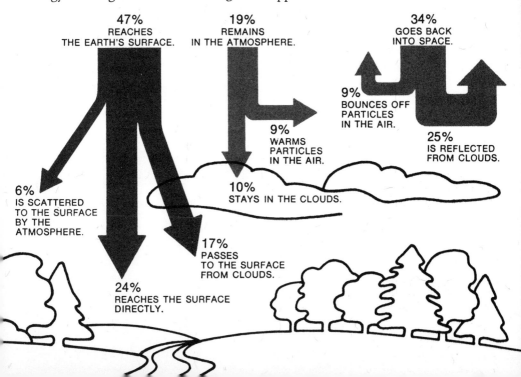

47%
REACHES
THE EARTH'S SURFACE.

19%
REMAINS
IN THE ATMOSPHERE.

34%
GOES BACK
INTO SPACE.

9%
BOUNCES OFF
PARTICLES
IN THE AIR.

9%
WARMS
PARTICLES
IN THE AIR.

25%
IS REFLECTED
FROM CLOUDS.

6%
IS SCATTERED
TO THE SURFACE
BY THE
ATMOSPHERE.

10%
STAYS IN THE CLOUDS.

17%
PASSES
TO THE SURFACE
FROM CLOUDS.

24%
REACHES THE SURFACE
DIRECTLY.

on our planet. In part, the 19 percent absorbed by the atmosphere is what creates these changes. Mostly, however, they are caused by the huge amounts of energy absorbed by the dry land and the oceans, as well as what is trapped by the blanketing effect of the atmosphere. The sun's radiation is stronger at the equator than at the poles. As a result, tropical air becomes warmed by radiation from the ground and rises. As it does so, the cooler polar air flows down and replaces it. These currents of air continually circulate around the earth, and their flow is always being disturbed by the earth's rotation and local changes in the atmosphere. The interaction of all these forces on one another produces the movement of air we call wind. Man has used the wind for centuries to power his sailing vessels and windmills. In addition, our weather cycles on earth produce much potential power in swiftly flowing rivers and streams. Man has learned to tap this source of power in hydroelectric stations to generate electricity.

Solar energy, falling upon the earth for millions and millions of years, is responsible for our fossil fuels—oil, coal, and natural gas. These fuels are literally the remains of animal and plant life, long ago buried and subjected to great pressures within the earth until they were chemically transformed into the products that man digs and drills for today to power his machinery and heat his buildings. But having blithely and wastefully used up much of this precious energy provided by the earth, man now finds that sources are either in short supply or difficult to obtain and that the cost of refining and transporting them is immense. Moreover, the fuel supplies that are left are often controlled by nations, which, for one political reason or another, are not always prepared to share them with the rest of the world.

Thus modern man, finding himself in a shrinking energy market, must seek new sources of energy. One alternative source, already being used today on a small scale but having great potential for the future, is solar energy. The attractions of solar energy are many. In a monetary sense, solar energy costs nothing; it is free for the taking and will not run out for billions of years. It doesn't pollute or otherwise damage the environment. It creates no dangerous waste products such as plutonium. It cannot be rationed or embargoed by any nation or people, nor can it be easily controlled by industrial cartels. Finally, the technology involved in obtaining energy from sunshine, while still not perfected, is much less complex than that needed to produce nuclear energy. Surely, if man can successfully harness the sun's enormous potential power, he need never again suffer energy shortages.

CHAPTER TWO

PIONEERS OF SOLAR ENERGY

Since ancient times man has recognized that solar radiation could be a very effective source of energy. Many of the past attempts to put sunlight to work involved collecting the sun's rays and focusing them to produce high temperatures. For centuries it has been known that a simple magnifying glass will concentrate the light of the sun into a beam so hot that it will cause wood to catch fire. A number of such burning glasses, not unlike children's toys of today, have been found in the ruins of ancient Nineveh and date from the seventh century B.C.

In the Greek comedy *The Clouds* by Aristophanes, one of the characters speaks of focusing a burning glass on a wax tablet as a means of wiping out some written evidence. And there is the story of the great Greek mathematician Archimedes, who, as an old man, invented a number of devices to prevent the capture of his native city, Syracuse, by invading Romans. One of them was supposed to have been a battery of cleverly arranged mirrors, which concentrated the sun's rays on the sails of Roman ships and set them afire. Whether or not this event actually happened is controversial, for no proof of it exists. Nevertheless, later scientists have all agreed that it could have been done.

While Galileo was examining the heavens with his crude telescope in the early 1600's, another man was successfully tinkering with one of the first solar-energy machines. He was the French engineer Salomon de Caus, who had learned how to concentrate the sun's rays to operate a small water pump. A few years later a German writer named Athanasius Kircher described in a book what may have been the first solar furnace. It was used to distill, or purify, water. A bowl-shaped mirror focused the sun's rays, which then heated the water in a flask. When the water had been sufficiently heated, some of it vaporized and condensed into a nearby jar, leaving the impurities in the flask.

Two brilliant pioneer chemists of the 1700's both regularly employed solar energy in their experiments. Joseph Priestley, discoverer of oxygen, first produced that basic element by heating oxide of mercury with a burning lens. And Antoine Lavoisier of France, often called the "father of chemistry," built a solar furnace with two immense lenses to focus the sun's rays. Lavoisier's furnace could reach temperatures as high as 2000 degrees Fahrenheit.

In the late 1860's, a French engineer named Auguste Mouchot developed a steam engine powered by the sun. It was used successfully to pump water in the French colony of Algeria. A few years later Mouchot built a much larger

15

The two-lensed solar furnace used by the French chemist Antoine Lavoisier in the late 1700's. *Burndy Library*

version of the engine, which was tested for several months in a water-distillation plant. Unfortunately, the French Government, which had backed his efforts, decided that his engines were too costly to warrant further support.

The Swedish-American engineer, John Ericsson, who gained fame during the Civil War for his Union ship, the ironclad *Monitor,* had been building highly successful hot-air engines for many years. After the war, he turned to making them run on solar energy or, as Ericsson put it, "the big fire hot enough to work engines at a distance of ninety million miles." By the mid-1870's, he had built eight (some of which can be seen today at the American-Swedish Historical Society in Philadelphia), but none of them were efficient enough for practical use.

One of the greatest pioneering uses of solar energy was an amazingly large solar-distillation plant built at Las Salinas in northern Chile in 1871 by an American named Charles Wilson. Its purpose was to make fresh water for use at a nitrate mine. In principle it was not unlike the early device described by Kircher, with water first being vaporized and then condensed, except of course that it did not employ a curved mirror to focus the sun's rays. Instead, the Las Salinas still was built with slanting roofs of glass over shallow pans of salt water, a method that continues to be used in various parts of the world today. Heat from the sun evaporated part of the seawater in the pans, and the vapor thus formed condensed on the inside surfaces of the slanting glass roofs, while salt remained dissolved in the rest of the seawater. The newly formed fresh water, rolling down the inside of the glass roofs, was then collected in troughs. This remarkably efficient solar still produced up to 6000 gallons of fresh water

The famous solar still built in the Andes Mountains at Las Salinas, Chile, over a century ago.   *Solar Energy Society*

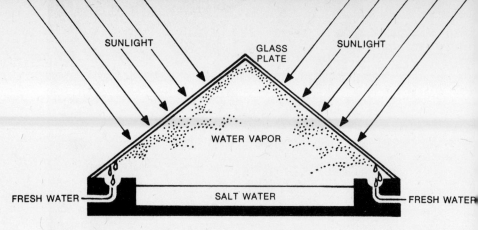

Solar energy is used to obtain fresh water from salt water. The sun's heat vaporizes the water, which condenses on the slanting glass, leaving the salt.

a day, and it operated successfully for forty years, until the nitrate mine was exhausted.

In the late 1870's, a French experimenter named Abel Pifre built a solar steam engine with a 100-foot dish-shaped collector to gather the sun's rays. Pifre's engine, which generated less than one horsepower, was one of the first to be used in a business venture. He operated a small printing press with it and published a newspaper appropriately called *Le Journal du Soleil,* or *The Sun Journal.* Pifre's solar engine, efficiently running the press, was exhibited at the World Exposition in Paris in 1878, and it turned out to be one of the hits of the show.

About this same time, another French innovator, Charles Tellier, constructed a solar engine that departed from those being built by other men. Instead of focusing the sun's rays

Artist's sketch of Abel Pifre's solar engine, which powered a small printing press at the Paris Exposition in 1878.

for heat, Tellier used what is now called a "flat-plate" collecting system. Its approximately 200 square feet of area gathered heat from the sunshine falling on it and imparted this heat to piping filled with a working fluid, which in turn drove the engine.

Meanwhile, solar experimenters in various countries had been building the first solar ovens for cooking food. For the most part these ovens were little more than simple containers with glass lids to admit sunlight and trap it inside. The indefatigable Auguste Mouchot demonstrated one at the 1878 Paris Exposition and was able to cook a pound of beef with it in less than half an hour. Better models were made after the turn of the century, using polished bowl-shaped mirrors to focus the solar radiation, by such men as Samuel Pierpont Langley and Charles Greeley Abbot.

In the early 1880's, in what was to be his last attempt, John Ericsson made a large engine designed to produce steam or air and powered by sunshine. For a collector he used a 175-square-foot curved mirror that focused the sun's rays to create high temperatures. The engine was used to operate a small pump, and Ericsson claimed that it delivered two horsepower. But he became discouraged with the economic future of solar

John Ericsson's celebrated sun motor erected at New York in 1883. A cylindrical mirror concentrated the sun's rays at the topmost member in the drawing, providing heat to run the engine. *Burndy Library*

power, lamenting the fact that although sunshine might be free, the equipment involved to harness it was costly. A canny businessman, Ericsson put aside his solar dream and converted his engines to run on conventional fuels such as coal and gas. Soon he was selling thousands of his engines throughout the world.

Around the turn of the century, a number of large solar engines were constructed. Some were highly successful while others quickly faded from the scene, due either to poor design or lack of funds for further research. One of the more successful inventors was a man named A.G. Eneas, who, with a few associates, set up a large solar-powered pump in the Arizona Territory near present-day Tempe in 1900. The following year a local newspaper in nearby Phoenix published an interesting description of the queer-looking contraption:

The unique feature of the solar motor is that it uses the heat of the sun to produce steam. . . . When the solar rays have heated the water in the boiler so as to produce steam, the remainder of the process is the familiar operation of compound engine and centrifugal pump.

The reflector somewhat resembles a huge umbrella, open and inverted at such an angle as to receive the full effect of the sun's rays on 1788 little mirrors lining its inside surface. . . . The boiler is the focal point where the reflection of the sun is concentrated. If you reach a long pole up to the boiler, it instantly begins to smoke and in a few seconds is aflame. From the boiler a flexible metallic pipe runs to the engine house near at hand. The reflector

The solar-powered pump built by A. G. Eneas in Arizona Territory in 1900.

is thirty-three and a half feet in diameter at the top and fifteen feet at the bottom. On the whole, its appearance is rather stately and graceful, and the glittering mirrors and shining boiler make it decidedly brilliant. . . .

Eneas was able to move the device about to different sites in the desert and successfully pumped irrigation water with it. Later, when he tried to promote and market his engines, which sold for about $2500, he failed for a number of reasons. For one thing, his original engine was sadly damaged by wind storms; for another, his models at other sites were constantly dogged by accidents and breakdowns.

Other inventors—two using a flat-plate system around 1905 —met with similar failure. All of these men proved time and again that devices using solar energy would work. However, they were innovators who were ahead of their time, and their ideas did not catch on sufficiently for widespread acceptance.

Yet one young engineer, a Pennsylvanian named Frank Shuman, came close to having total success in his solar-energy ventures. In 1907, Shuman, using a flat-plate collector, built a test steam engine that generated a praiseworthy 3½ horsepower. Encouraged by the success of this model, Shuman began to dream of an immense four-acre collector system that would power an equally large steam plant. This gigantic project was intended to run a series of turbines continuously and produce 1000 horsepower. However, Shuman decided that the technological limitations of his day made the idea impractical, and he turned to other things.

Deciding that he must use focused sunlight for greater heat, Shuman's next solar collector consisted of some two dozen sheet-metal troughs, which were actually mirrors curved so that they would reflect the sun's heat onto boilers. With them, he hoped to develop as much as 100 horsepower. At least, that was Shuman's dream as he worked many long months to complete the solar steam plant at its site in a small town near Philadelphia. When at last it was finished, the young engineer had spent $20,000 on the project—an appreciable sum in 1908.

Though Shuman's plant did not come close to producing the 100 horsepower, it still worked well—while the sun shone. When it didn't, or when industrial pollution blocked

This solar engine, built by Frank Shuman in 1907, used a flat-plate collector system.

out the sun's rays, the plant's operating ability was cut to zero. Actually, this setback did not bother Frank Shuman because he had designed his plant to operate under sunnier skies than those of Pennsylvania. Already he had formed a company of his own, the Sun Power Company, and he had obtained funds from English backers for a joint venture to be called the Eastern Sun Power Company, Limited, of London. With technical aid supplied by his British friends, Shuman soon obtained permission to build a solar plant in Egypt. By 1912, it was in efficient operation at Meadi, a suburb of Cairo.

While Shuman's Pennsylvania solar plant was well designed, his Meadi model was even more so, despite the reduction of collectors from twenty-six to only seven. For one thing, he had redesigned the collectors in a dish shape, which enabled them to focus the sun's rays more effectively. In addition, Shuman had spaced them farther apart so that one would not cast a shadow on the next and cut down its efficiency. Each was over 200 feet long, and Shuman had ingeniously designed them with special gearing systems so that they would follow the sun automatically as it arced across the blue Egyptian sky.

It was a nervous moment for Frank Shuman and his co-workers when they first put the plant into operation. But they all had the satisfaction of seeing it start to pump water from the Nile River inland for irrigation. Although the plant never delivered the 100 horsepower its designer had hoped for, it did produce a steady 52—and never fell below that mark. Once, in fact, it climbed to a high rating of 63.

Unfortunately for Shuman—and for the future of solar energy—the Meadi plant remained in operation for only a few months. The irrigation work done by Shuman's plant normally was performed by thousands of Egyptian laborers, and labor disputes regularly hampered the running of the plant. Eventually, with the disruption caused by the approach of World War I and other problems, Frank Shuman sadly abandoned his brilliantly conceived solar plant and saw it fall all too quickly into disrepair.

A few years after Shuman's ill-starred project at Meadi, the first attempt to store solar-generated energy was made in New Mexico by an engineer named Harrington. Sunlight was focused on a boiler that ran a steam engine. The engine pumped water twenty feet high into a 5000-gallon storage tank from where it ran down through a water turbine that operated a small dynamo. The electricity produced was enough to light an entire mine.

But the future of solar energy was dealt a great blow by the advent of World War I. The need for the nations involved to run their war machines brought a seemingly inexhaustible flow of cheap oil and gas from the Middle East and elsewhere. As long as these fossil fuels remained plentiful and easy to obtain, it was considerably more profitable to use them than to try to utilize the energy in sunshine.

Thus, solar energy once again became the province of tinkerers and dreamers, finding practical use in only a handful of specialized applications. Only in the 1930's did modern

Dr. Charles Greeley Abbot, father of solar-energy research in the United States, demonstrates one of his solar stoves.

research on the use of solar energy commence in earnest. Developments included the invention, in 1936, of a remarkably efficient solar boiler by Charles Greeley Abbot. Dr. Abbot, though often called the father of solar-energy research in the United States, was actually a brilliant astrophysicist working at the Smithsonian Institution. His reputation rests not so much on his practical accomplishments with solar devices as on his pioneering studies of the sun itself, notably his work in cataloging the solar spectrum.

In the 1930's, too, programs of study in solar energy were started at a few forward-looking universities. Later an experimental solar home or two was built, and a few desalinization plants were attempted.

During World War II, small solar-still "survival kits," designed by Dr. Maria Telkes, were used by the United States Navy. In the mid-1950's, brilliant breakthrough research was done at the Bell Telephone Laboratories in developing the solar battery. And simultaneously, the Association for Applied Solar Energy (AFASE) was formed by a group of distinguished scientific, academic, industrial, financial, and agricultural leaders to stimulate research on greater utilization of solar energy. But, for the most part, the public and world governments remained largely indifferent to the possibilities of solar power until the energy shortages of the 1970's.

CHAPTER THREE

COLLECTING THE SUN'S HEAT

Why has it taken man so long to utilize the sun's light for energy purposes? One reason is that the energy contained in sunshine is diffuse, or spread out, compared to the concentrated energy found in fossil fuels. For example, it would take many square feet of sunlight, properly collected and tapped from a suitable surface, to equal the concentrated energy contained in a handful of coal.

Capturing sunlight and putting it to work is particularly difficult because the solar energy that reaches the earth is spread out over a large area. The sun simply does not deliver much energy to any one place at any one time. In fact, the rate at which a location on earth receives solar energy depends on a number of conditions. These include the time of day, the season of the year, the latitude of the area, and the clearness or cloudiness of the sky.

Furthermore, the amount of solar energy received varies because of changes in the earth's orbit and the tilt of its spin axis. (The extent of this tilt, of course, determines the extent of seasonal changes.) There are also slight variations in the amount of energy radiated by the sun itself. These variations follow the eleven-year sunspot cycle and relate chiefly to ultraviolet radiation. (Sunspots are dark areas on the surface of the sun thought to be associated with magnetic storm activity.)

In the United States, the all-weather, day-and-night daily average rate at which sunlight falls on each square foot of the earth's surface is only about twenty watts. And in the tropics, where the sun is directly overhead at noon, the amount is not much more. Such a small amount of energy, unless it is somehow collected and put to a practical use, will simply dissipate into the air or the ground and be lost.

For this reason the sun's radiation, to be of any practical use, must be collected and concentrated by various devices known as solar-energy collectors. If the rays of the sun are concentrated by a collector at a single point, the temperature at that point rises. Therefore, the temperature of any substance placed at that point also is raised. A concave mirror— one that curves inward like a bowl—is a good collector of solar energy and can be used to operate a solar cooker.

A simple solar cooker can easily be made with a number of small mirrors, each one or two inches square. The mirrors are fastened to a board, tilted in a position so that the total effect is of a single concave mirror. The board itself is tilted to face the sun, as shown in the illustration. Sunlight strikes the mirrors and is reflected to a pan, which thus becomes hot enough to cook food.

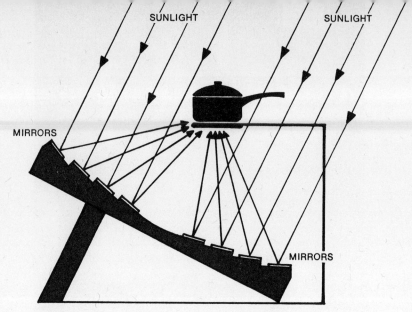

A simple solar cooker.

Solar cookers can be made to cook food either by concentrating the sun's rays directly on the cooking utensil or on a container holding a liquid and then circulating the heated liquid through a cooking oven. The direct solar cooker is a simple and efficient unit, but since it operates only while the sun is shining, its practicality is limited. Nevertheless, in areas of the world such as the Middle East, where the sun shines nearly every day, solar cookers are in daily use. Some of them can develop temperatures up to 350 degrees Fahrenheit, hot enough to boil a quart of water in fifteen minutes. They can broil, fry, or even pressure-cook, depending on the apparatus that is assembled at the focusing point of the sun's rays.

An Indian woman demonstrates a solar cooker of the type mass-produced in India a few years ago.

The solar furnace operates on the same principle as the small solar cooker, but on a much grander scale. This device, which has long been used in scientific investigation, produces a very high concentration of focused solar radiation. Its great advantage is that it can be heated to extremely high temperatures. Large, highly polished, curved mirrors make the best collectors. However, because of the enormous cost of

31

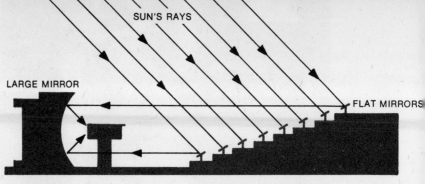

SUN'S RAYS

LARGE MIRROR

FLAT MIRRORS

In the solar furnace at Font-Romeu, France, the sun's rays enter the furnace from arrays of flat mirrors placed on a nearby hillside. The mirrors turn to follow the sun and reflect the rays on the large mirror.

these mirrors, large solar furnaces are made by mounting smaller glass mirrors on a large curved frame and adjusting each mirror to hit a central focal spot.

High in the Pyrenees Mountains of southern France, near a small village called Mont-Louis, French engineers led by Dr. Felix Trombe constructed a successful solar furnace after World War II. One of the reasons for its success is that Mont-Louis has an average of 250 days of sunshine a year; another is the ingenuity of Felix Trombe in setting up the furnace. The sun's rays enter the furnace—actually a small building holding the objects to be heated—from arrays of flat mirrors terraced on a nearby hillside. The mirrors turn to follow the sun as it moves across the sky, so they can reflect the sun's rays on a large mirror consisting of 3500 tiny mirrors arranged in a giant bowl. This huge collector in turn concentrates the rays on a much smaller concave mirror, which refocuses them on the object to be melted in the furnace. The furnace can reach temperatures of nearly 6000 degrees Fahrenheit and can melt through a thick iron bar in about fifteen seconds. An even larger furnace built by Trombe at Font-Romeu, France, can develop temperatures of over 9000 degrees Fahrenheit, nearly as hot as the surface of the sun itself. Maintenance of the mirror system is usually done at night, since the sun's rays can incinerate a person within seconds, even on overcast days.

A smaller solar furnace, in Denver, Colorado, can produce temperatures up to 3600 degrees Fahrenheit. Its collector is a huge bowl-shaped mirror measuring forty-five feet across and mounted on a rotating frame so that the instrument can be

The solar furnace at Font-Romeu, showing the giant parabolic mirror, which focuses the sun's rays onto the smaller building in front of it. The structure that houses the large mirror is actually an office building. At left is one of the turnable small mirrors on the nearby hillside.

Centre National de la Recherche Scientifique

turned to follow the sun. Currently it is being used to study the application of solar energy in spacecraft.

Solar engineers know that the highest temperatures can be attained by using directional collectors like those at Denver and Mont-Louis. They are designed to follow the sun across the sky from sunrise to sunset in order to obtain the maximum intensity of the sun's rays. However, the machinery necessary to tilt and angle arrays of such collectors precisely is complex and expensive. Also, polished, curved solar mirrors of whatever material are costly to manufacture. Thus many solar engineers prefer to work with less-expensive flat-plate collectors.

In its simplest form, a flat-plate collector consists of a metal plate painted black on the side that faces the sun. Black absorbs sunlight more effectively than any other color. The sunlight absorbed by the plate heats it. The heat produced by the solar energy is removed for use by circulating water or some other working fluid through pipes attached to the underside of the metal plate. To prevent loss of heat from the plate, the underside is carefully insulated in the areas that have no pipes. A sheet of glass is usually attached to the front, about an inch from the black surface. The glass and the one-inch air space act as further insulators to guard against heat loss once the metal plate has become hot. Flat-plate collectors have been used to heat houses and to distill fresh water from seawater.

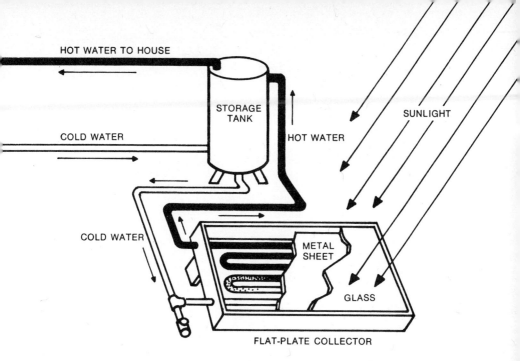

HOT WATER TO HOUSE

STORAGE TANK

COLD WATER

HOT WATER

SUNLIGHT

COLD WATER

METAL SHEET

GLASS

FLAT-PLATE COLLECTOR

A flat-plate collector as it is used to operate a solar water heater.

Flate-plate collectors are also used in solar water heaters. Such heaters work well in regions that receive a great deal of sunshine most of the year. They are generally installed on the roofs of houses, and many are found in the United States, in Florida and Arizona, and in Israel.

The solar water heater shown in the diagram is typical of those in operation today. When the flat-plate collector becomes hot enough to heat water, a device called a "thermostat" causes a pump to start operating. Water begins to circulate from a storage tank through the collector pipes, often arranged in coils, and then back again to the tank. Eventually

A solar water heater mounted on a rooftop in Israel.

Israeli Tourist Bureau

the tank, which is well insulated to prevent heat loss, becomes
a small reservoir of heated water. This hot water may then
be piped to a faucet or to a radiator for heating the house.

Flat-plate collectors, though not directional, continue to
operate reasonably well on hazy or cloudy days. (Some solar
energy penetrates the earth's surface even on overcast days.)
Yet while solar energy trapped with flat-plate collectors may
be adequate for heating purposes in homes, it can heat a
working fluid to only about 400 degrees Fahrenheit, which
is too low to operate solar boilers. These devices are ones in
which water is heated and converted to steam to operate ma-

36

chinery. Such low-temperature solar energy cannot compete with fossil-fuel power plants, which operate most efficiently with steam at close to 1000 degrees. So one of the main disadvantages of flat-plate collectors is simply that no steam turbines have been developed that will run on the low temperatures they produce.

To get higher temperatures—about 600 degrees Fahrenheit —engineers can bend flat-plate collectors into trough-shaped concentrators like those used by pioneer Frank Shuman. Though the temperature of 600 degrees is still lower than the steam temperatures produced in fossil-fuel plants, it is comparable to those produced in nuclear plants. Presently, in a National Science Foundation research program, the University of Minnesota and Honeywell, Inc., are developing troughs four feet across and eight feet long to focus sunlight on pipes covered with a coating of aluminum oxide in which water is heated.

To boost steam temperatures to 1000 degrees Fahrenheit and beyond, further concentration of the sun's light is necessary, and the fixed-trough approach is no longer adequate. To achieve these temperatures, solar engineers believe that directional, bowl-shaped mirrors such as those employed in the Pyrenees will be necessary. In fact, a solar-thermal power plant called the "central receiver," supported by the National Science Foundation resembles the French design.

The central receiver, already on the designers' drawing

Artist's sketch of trough-shaped solar-energy collectors to be built by Honeywell, Inc., and University of Minnesota personnel for experimentation with a central power station in Arizona.   *Honeywell, Inc.*

boards, consists of hundreds of automatically pointed collectors distributed around a central tower. Sunlight is focused on the top of the tower where heat is absorbed by a working fluid, which is then carried below to make steam to operate machinery for heating, lighting, air conditioning, and so forth. This central receiver would require a square mile of reflectors and a central tower 1500 feet high.

New communities, new shopping centers, and new clusters of commercial buildings are constantly springing up all over the United States and other countries. These centers of activity customarily require from 100 to 300 megawatts (one megawatt equals one million watts) of power for heating

38

and electrical requirements. The ratio between these heating and electrical needs is about seven to one, essentially the same as that in the output of a solar-thermal power plant of the central-receiver type. In other words, the outputs of solar-thermal power plants are well matched to the power needs of these groups of buildings. And, in the view of the Na-

Artist's concept of a solar-energy central receiver system. Hundreds of steerable mirrors focus the sun's reflected energy on water in the solar, or central, tower. The heated water is converted into steam and returned to the ground to drive steam turbine electrical generators.

McDonnell Douglas Corp.

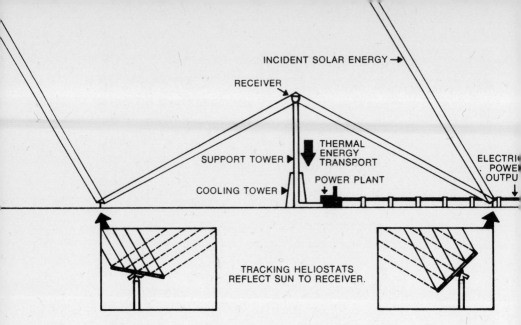

INCIDENT SOLAR ENERGY →

RECEIVER

THERMAL
ENERGY
TRANSPORT

SUPPORT TOWER ►

ELECTRIC
POWER
OUTPU

POWER PLANT

COOLING TOWER ►

TRACKING HELIOSTATS
REFLECT SUN TO RECEIVER.

A schematic view of the total solar-energy central receiver system. Such installations for solar-thermal conversion may be in common use about year 2000. *McDonnell Douglas Corp.*

tional Science Foundation, such places will prove ideal for the creation of new solar designs that will achieve remarkably high efficiencies in using the sun's heat.

Solar engineers have a term for the method of using solar energy to drive turbines that generate electricity on a large scale. It is called "solar-thermal conversion." Research in this important area is currently being conducted under National Science Foundation grants by such organizations as Westinghouse, the Aerospace Corporation of Los Angeles, Honeywell, Inc., and the University of Arizona. In addition, a few electric utilities, realizing the great potential of the sun in their vital services, are privately funding research in solar-thermal conversion.

Meanwhile, until solar-thermal conversion becomes a reality, the sun's heat is being harnessed and used in more conventional ways around the world. For instance, Japan, which imports over 90 percent of its fuel, has adopted one of the most ambitious programs for integrating solar installations into its economy. Solar water heaters are already being mass-produced and are in common use, and the Government is encouraging the development of solar-produced hydrogen as a fuel. The Soviet Union, with its vast undeveloped territories, has concentrated on introducing solar devices that will help tame the wilderness, such as solar-powered sluice gates for remote irrigation ditches and a still that provides sheep with fresh water from brine lying deep beneath the desert.

In San Francisco, a salt company literally makes salt with sunshine. Using vast salt pans that cover several acres, the company can precipitate—separate out—four inches of salt crystals a year from seawater by evaporation. An ancient process, salt drying is less economical than mining solid salt, but such evaporators currently produce a million tons a year in the United States.

Solar stills for purifying water, most of them experimental at present, are nevertheless in rather wide use in the warmer parts of the world. One was constructed at Puerto Peñasco, Mexico, by the University of Arizona and the University of

Sonora. Its 12,000-square-foot collectors produce, by evaporation and condensation, about 6000 gallons of fresh water every day. On a number of Greek islands solar stills are an important source of fresh water for the inhabitants. Others are in operation in Florida, California, and the Middle East.

The future of solar energy looks especially bright in Australia. Here is an entire continent whose climate is largely tropical or subtropical and whose skies are clear and sunny much of the year. Solar water heaters are widely used in Australia today. Moreover, intensive solar-energy research is being conducted there, as sponsored by the Commonwealth Scientific and Industrial Research Organization (CSIRO). There is a large solar still located at Coober Pedy and a prototype of a high-temperature water heater at Griffith. Engineers at CSIRO have even built a prototype of a solar timber kiln whose air heaters, utilizing collected heat from the sun, speed the drying-out process in lumber production.

Solar scientists and engineers agree that the focus for the immediate future is on solar heating. But they do not mean a few solar cookers here and there, or several hundred solar water heaters mounted atop houses, or large-scale production

opposite, top: A commercial solar water heater, with flat-plate collectors atop a hotel in Darwin, Australia. *center:* The solar still at Coober Pedy, Australia. *bottom:* A solar timber kiln in Australia used for drying green lumber.
Commonwealth Scientific and Industrial Research Organization

of solar furnaces for industrial purposes. Nor do they believe that the highly promising solar-thermal conversion plants are just around the corner; with luck, the first of them will be coming into use in the last decade of this century. Rather these specialists are talking about using solar energy *now* for heating (and cooling) the spaces in which we do most of our living—houses and buildings.

CHAPTER FOUR

SOLAR HOUSES AND BUILDINGS

In the field of architecture, one basic principle of solar heating is far from new. The Greek historian Xenophon noted as early as 400 B.C., "We should build the south side of houses loftier, to get the winter sun, and the north side lower to keep out the cold winds." The Roman architect Vitruvius, in the first century B.C., devoted much of his writings to similar suggestions on building designs for various climates and locales.

Had Xenophon and Vitruvius lived closer to the equatorial tropics, they would not have been concerned about heating their homes, for in a few favored spots on the globe the sun and weather combine to create a perpetual Eden. Elsewhere, of course, in the more temperate latitudes of Europe, North America, and China, where most of the world's population dwells, man must collect and then burn fossil fuels for heating (and cooling) in order to balance the excesses and deficiencies of climate.

But nearly everywhere—except in the higher latitudes of the earth—the sun provides enough energy to do much of the job. The so-called solar belt extends from the equator north and south to the fortieth parallels of latitude. Thus, solar devices—including solar houses—work well in most of the populated areas of the world. Naturally, the more sunshine, the more efficient the device, since the sun when high overhead is stronger than when it is low on the horizon. But even as far north as Montreal, a solar house has proved efficient. In fact, studies have shown that houses located in regions of cold winters and large amounts of winter sunshine are best suited to solar heating, although some kind of auxiliary source of heat must be used when extended sunless periods occur.

The National Science Foundation has stated that in sunny, temperate climates the sun can provide three quarters of the heating and cooling needs of a 1500-square-foot home using from 600 to 800 square feet of the roof for a collector surface. Scientists at the National Science Foundation further predict that if solar heating and cooling equipment were built into all new homes and single-story commercial buildings in the United States between now and the year 2000, the sun would meet 4.5 percent of the country's overall energy needs and, by the year 2020, probably 8 percent. These percentages would mean significant savings indeed, and enough technology already exists to begin using sunshine to provide such heating and cooling.

To accomplish this goal, however, architects would have to revise their methods for constructing buildings to accommodate the equipment needed to utilize solar energy. Already existing structures would have to be adapted to such equipment. For example, the roof of a typical American home could be adapted to receive energy collectors, even though it is now built for the opposite purpose: to exclude solar radiation.

A modern solar home in Columbus, Ohio. Rooftop solar-collector cells face south to capture sunlight in an absorber plate. Solar energy is then transferred to a working fluid connected with heating, cooling, and hot-water systems.   *PPG Industries, Inc.*

Essentially, a solar home requires three basic components for both heating and cooling. First, there must be a solar-heat collector, which can be a heat-absorbing surface that transfers the heat to some working fluid such as water. Second, a heat reservoir is needed. It is usually a thermally (heat) insulated container in the basement, filled with water or some other heat absorber such as crushed rock. A reservoir may not be needed if some other back-up energy system is used. Third, there must be an air conditioner using an engine or motor that runs on solar heat. Actually, the air-conditioning part of the system lags behind the heating technology a bit, and more research must be done to improve it. Nevertheless, solar air conditioning is operating today in a few experimental buildings.

In addition, there would be the necessary pumps and valves that would control the flow of the working fluid to and from the heat reservoir. The reservoir ensures that the roof-collected heat is available when and where it is needed and stored for later use when it is not needed. The stored heat can be applied to both winter heating and summer cooling and provide hot water when it is needed. A conventional auxiliary heater would be used when the sun and stored heat cannot provide enough energy, with the amount of auxiliary heat depending on climate and weather.

The principle of solar-home heating is simple and basically is the same as that of the solar water heater, except that the

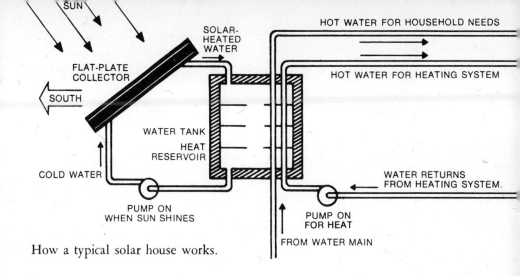

How a typical solar house works.

object is not just to heat water but also the family living areas. As one solar engineer put it, "The use of solar collectors and heat-storage systems is more of a plumbing problem than an engineering problem." Let's see how a typical solar-heated house works.

In one of its simplest forms, a solar house uses flat-plate collectors mounted on the rooftop facing south. The collectors are usually in the form of a box or boxes containing black-coated water pipes over a black surface. One or several layers of glass over the box permit the sunlight to enter but keep the radiant heat emitted by the pipes and black surface from escaping into the atmosphere. The water in the pipes is heated by the sun and is circulated through the house by a small pump. The heated water is stored in a heavily insulated tank (the heat reservoir) where it can retain its heat for one to four or five days. The tank would thus furnish heat at

49

night or when the sun is clouded over. Some plans call for the heated water to run through a series of coils in a hot-air duct containing a fan that blows the heat into the various rooms of the house, as in a conventional hot-air heating system. In other installations air is circulated directly over the black collector plates and distributed around the house.

Until quite recently there were only about two dozen houses in the United States that were heated by the sun; today their number is steadily increasing. In 1975, a Harvard physicist completed a world study of solar buildings and reported that there were 138 solar-heated structures in the world, which included 85 solar-heated houses in the United States.

Most of the earlier models were experimental, and some turned out to be more efficient than others. Between 1939 and 1958, a major research program at the Massachusetts Institute of Technology was conducted to develop energy collectors for homes. Test houses were built, the last one at Lexington, Massachusetts, in 1958. This two-story house was equipped with 640 square feet of metal and glass solar-collector panels on a south-sloping roof. Deriving heat from the store in a 1500-gallon water tank, the forced-air system supplied a little over 50 percent of the heating demand.

opposite: The pioneer solar home at Lexington, Massachusetts, built by the Massachusetts Institute of Technology, and a cutaway view showing its operation.   *M.I.T.*

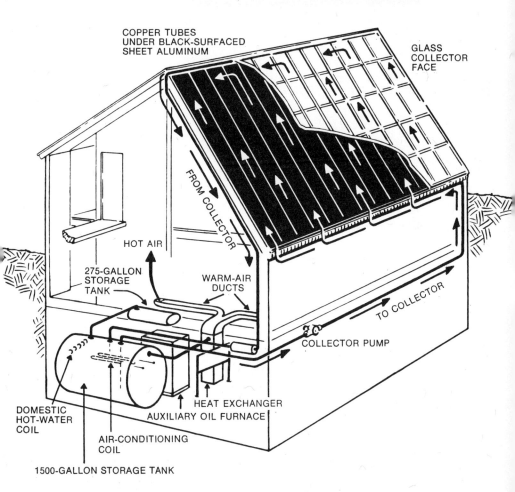

COPPER TUBES
UNDER BLACK-SURFACED
SHEET ALUMINUM

GLASS
COLLECTOR
FACE

FROM COLLECTOR

HOT AIR

275-GALLON
STORAGE
TANK

WARM-AIR
DUCTS

TO COLLECTOR

COLLECTOR PUMP

DOMESTIC
HOT-WATER
COIL

AIR-CONDITIONING
COIL

HEAT EXCHANGER
AUXILIARY OIL FURNACE

1500-GALLON STORAGE TANK

The home of solar-house pioneer Harry E. Thomason in suburban Washington, D.C. At left is the solarium containing a solar-heated swimming pool.

Federal Energy Research and Development Administration

One leading solar engineer, Dr. George Löf of Colorado State University, built two houses using solar heating in the late 1950's. He is now constructing a third under a grant from the National Science Foundation. Löf's older houses get only about 33 percent of their heating needs from sunshine, because of undersized collectors and storage area, but his newest solar home is expected to perform with greater efficiency.

Perhaps America's best known solar-home pioneer is a man named Harry F. Thomason. He is not an engineer at all, but a former attorney, and he has built three solar-heated houses in the Washington, D.C., area. Thomason claims that all three of his houses can use sunshine to provide an amazing

90 percent of their heating needs, making his solar homes by far the most successful in the world. His first, built in 1959, operated on sunlight during the coldest winter Washington had known in forty-three years, and the family living in it paid only about six dollars for auxiliary oil heat.

Thomason himself lives in one of his solar houses. An apparatus that he built collects solar heat on his roof and carries it to his basement, where it is stored in a 1600-gallon tank of water surrounded by stones for insulation. When the

Another Thomason solar house built in 1975 in suburban Washington, D.C. The black-painted aluminum solar collectors will provide heat and air conditioning for this four-bedroom house.
Federal Energy Research and Development Administration

temperature in his house falls below 70 degrees, an electric blower automatically begins to circulate air through the warm stones and back upstairs until the temperature rises a few degrees. Thomason says that even on the coldest days his system collects some solar heat, and, he adds, if it weren't for clouds obscuring the sun he would not need an auxiliary oil heater at all. However, poor weather comes in spells, and after three or four cloudy days his solar house is forced to fall back on oil heat.

Because Thomason's system is not the work of a professional engineer, solar experts tend to regard it as amateur. Nevertheless, the apparent key to his success is the large size of the heat collectors and storage devices, made possible by the inexpensive materials he uses. Instead of using expensive copper or aluminum piping in his rooftop collector, he uses a sheet of black, corrugated aluminum. On top of the collector he bolts dozens of rectangles of cheap glass to retain the heat. Whenever the temperature of the aluminum sheet is warm enough, the system begins pumping reserve water from the basement to the roof, where it dribbles down the heated corrugated grooves into a gutter and back down into the basement tank. In good weather, the water downstairs remains at a temperature of about 85 to 95 degrees. The tank and the stones around it take up about a third of the basement.

An unusual experimental solar house has been completed at the University of Delaware's Institute of Energy Conversion. Funded in part by a grant from the National Science Foundation, it is called Solar One. The house utilizes solar-electric cells mounted on the roof to provide electricity by converting the sun's energy to electric current. Great pains were taken in the construction of Solar One to utilize most of the sunlight striking the house. Its south-facing, deeply slanted roof containing the collectors sets it apart in appearance from the usual suburban home, and its windows are rather narrow to permit better thermal insulation. Solar One does not have air conditioning powered by sunlight, but a similar experimental house, Solar Two, being completed at Colorado State University, will have.

Solar One, the experimental solar house at the University of Delaware, has cadmium sulfide cells on the roof to generate electricity, as well as thermal collectors to provide energy for heating.

University of Delaware

Many solar engineers think that solar cooling actually offers a greater future potential than solar heating. The reason is that the sun is at its peak and hottest in the summer months when its energy is most needed to refrigerate and air-condition homes. The situation is reversed when sunshine is used for heating homes; that is, in the cooler months the sun is not at its zenith overhead and is not as hot. In fact, solar-refrigeration systems have already been built, and their feasibility has been demonstrated. But economics remain a stumbling block, for it is still cheaper to air-condition and refrigerate a house with gas or electricity. The answer lies in cutting costs to make solar-energy methods more competitive with fossil-fuel methods. Fortunately, many solar experts think that a breakthrough in materials and design could well make solar air conditioning practical in a few years.

A few solar houses include swimming pools in their heating systems, and hundreds of pools are being heated separately by homemade solar collectors. But a large collector area is needed, which sometimes poses architectural difficulties. Nevertheless, the attractiveness of heating pools by sunlight is obvious, for gas heaters are not only expensive initially but costly to operate.

New approaches to solar homes have been tried by a handful of innovative solar engineers. One of these men, Harold Hay, built a solar house in the late 1960's in Phoenix, Arizona. It used no conventional collectors on the roof but

This solar house, by Harold Hay, in Arizona uses no conventional collectors on the roof but movable roof panels, which alternately cover and expose shallow ponds of water for heat storage and cooling.

United Press International

movable roof panels, which alternately covered and exposed shallow ponds of water. In this simple solar-heated house, the uncovered ponds of water stored up the heat of the blazing Arizona sun by day; then, at night or during cloudy periods, the shallow tanks could be covered by the panels to prevent heat loss.

More recently, in cooperation with architects and engineers at California State Polytechnic College, Hay built a new solar house called Sky-Therm in Atascadero, California. The house roof is covered with clear plastic bags filled with water, similar in design to water beds. In winter, they gather and store heat for the house. At night, an insulated panel covers the water beds to prevent heat from escaping. During the summer, the process is reversed; the water beds are covered during the daytime and the insulating panels are removed at night to allow the heat from within the house to dissipate, cooling the interior.

Near Albuquerque, New Mexico, another solar engineer named Steven Baer has built several small houses using techniques of solar heating and cooling similar in principle to the Sky-Therm system. Baer's houses incorporate such low-cost features as the use of ordinary fifty-five-gallon drums for heat storage and skylights with insulating panels for additional heat.

At the Massachusetts Institute of Technology, architect Sean Wellesley-Miller and physicist Day Chahroudi are testing new materials. Chahroudi has designed an inexpensive solar-heated structure that he calls a "biosphere," which would contain a greenhouse for growing vegetables and plants. The biosphere would be built with a south-facing wall of a transparent plastic membrane that turns opaque in certain temperature ranges. In winter, the plastic surface would remain transparent only when the sun was shining and would turn opaque at other times to reduce the loss of heat; the process would be reversed during the summer. The two scientists contend that more than 80 percent of a typical home's heating needs could be supplied by using the plastic collectors and that an 800-square-foot greenhouse could pro-

Called the Decade 80 Solar House, this prototype, built in 1975 near Tucson, Arizona, uses solar energy for nearly 100 percent of its heating and 75 percent of its cooling.

Copper Development Association, Inc.

vide almost all of a family's fruit and vegetable needs yearly in the Northeastern United States.

In addition to those mentioned, there are today other solar-heated (and some solar-cooled) houses in New Mexico, California, Oregon, and Florida. Others are being built in several more states, including Nebraska, Arizona, Colorado, and Connecticut.

At a symposium on solar-energy techniques in Albany, New York, in 1975, a group of solar experts agreed that, in the area of home heating, the most efficient system is a solar-assist heat pump with conventional heating as a back-up. A heat-pump system uses the difference in temperature in the air inside and outside a structure, or within the earth deep beneath a structure, for heating and cooling. These systems are widely used in the Southwestern United States, and General Electric Company is now manufacturing them and promoting their use in the Northeast.

As for solar buildings other than dwelling houses, a surprising number are already planned for the near future. A New York engineering firm is working on plans for two solar-heated and -cooled Federal buildings, one scheduled to go up in Michigan and the other in New Hampshire. The National Science Foundation is funding and testing a variety of solar-energy structures across the United States, among which is the nation's largest solar project now under construction in Denver. It is to be a solar plant that will heat a 278,000-square-foot classroom center at Denver Community College. The total cost will be about $10,000,000, but its designers claim that with the rising cost of conventional fuel, it will pay for itself in ten years. Fuel costs for the new plant are, of course, zero.

Already on the drawing boards or under construction are such institutional projects as a new solar-heated conservatory and administration building for the New York Botanical Garden in Millbrook, New York. And the Massachusetts Audubon Society has commissioned Arthur D. Little, Inc., the industrial consulting firm, to design a solar-heating and -cooling system for its new library and office building in Lincoln, Massachusetts, with actual construction to begin as soon as possible. The firm estimates that the system will handle 65 to 85 percent of the heating load and 50 percent of the air-conditioning needs.

Arthur D. Little, Inc., is also conducting an important study

A solar skyscraper along the lines of this model is the ultimate goal of a project being financed by PPG Industries and several other firms. To be erected in Pittsburgh, Pennsylvania, the building's roof and windows on three sides will be angled to catch the sun's energy with collector cells. *PPG Industries, Inc.*

for some eighty commercial firms to define the technical, economic, and marketing prospects for future solar technology. So far, the study indicates that there is considerable market potential for solar-energy devices, especially the smaller home-heating kind that could be sold at a relatively low cost. Furthermore, the study indicates that commerical development of solar energy could be so rapid that in twenty years the saving in conventional fuel sources in the United States alone could equal two million barrels of oil a day—approximately the amount expected to flow through the Alaska pipeline.

Why, then, with the basic solar technology already available, with thousands of energy-conscious homeowners wanting to build solar homes, and with the fast-rising costs of oil, gas, and electricity, isn't solar heating a major factor in the marketplace right now? According to observers in the field, there are many reasons. The initial cost of solar-collector units is high, they are not readily available, and sales outlets for them are scarce.

For someone building a new solar-heated house, the cost of such solar-collector units would add between $2000 and $5000 to the overall cost of the home, depending on its size and other factors. Installing these units in older houses would be even more expensive. This initial outlay compares with the present cost of only $1000 to $2000 for a conventional furnace-heating system. Solar-energy advocates are quick to point

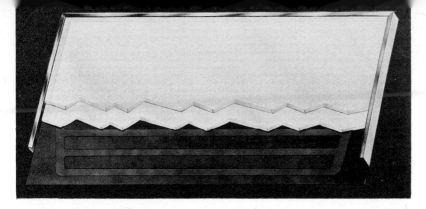

Modern solar-collector cells like this one are key components for solar-energy systems to provide hot water and heat for homes and buildings. The sealed unit has two glass panels for insulation and weather protection and a black aluminum absorber plate, backed by fiber glass insulation. Working fluid circulates in the cell's built-in tubing to carry the sun's heat. *PPG Industries, Inc.*

out, however, that over a twenty-year period solar heating would turn out to be cheaper in the long run because fuel costs would be eliminated. Still, prospective homeowners are hesitant to pay the added initial cost of the solar-heating units, and architects remain reluctant to change their designs to accommodate the units.

Solar-home engineers and designers use a rule of thumb: the area, in square feet, of the roof collectors needed to heat a house adequately should equal about a third of the dwelling's internal square footage. By this rule, a 1000-square-foot home would need some 330 square feet of solar collectors. Assuming that the collectors retailed for as low as $6 per square foot—as indeed the firm of PPG Industries of Pittsburgh plans to offer them eventually—the cost would be about $2000, not including the additional cost of shipping, plumbing, storage tank, and installation. The total outlay for solar heating a small house like this may not be staggering for people with higher incomes, but it is still far above the budgets of many.

Despite these obstacles, the prospects for the immediate future of solar heating are bright. The United States Government has already earmarked some $300,000,000 for solar-energy programs over the next three years and will probably allocate more. Two states presently offer reduced property-tax assessments for homeowners who buy and use solar-heating equipment. And bills are now before Congress proposing individual income-tax reductions up to $3000 to help defray the costs of installing solar units in homes.

To create more public confidence in solar heating as quickly as possible, National Science Foundation engineers have retro-fitted—adapted—four schools in Virginia, Maryland, Minnesota, and Massachusetts with solar-heating equipment. At two schools, the collectors are on the roof; at the other two they will be on the ground nearby. Not only is retrofitting quickly completed, but new data can also be gathered for the design of new solar-heated buildings. If the school structures turn out to be successful, the National Science Foundation thinks that thousands of similar ones, such as shopping centers and warehouses, can be quickly retrofitted to save energy. Perhaps most important, the four schools are all highly visible,

This junior high school in suburban Minneapolis has been retrofitted with an experimental solar-energy heating system. A working fluid circulated through the 246 collectors is heated by the sun and used to heat and return air from the school. *Honeywell, Inc.*

and people seeing them in successful operation will be impressed with the benefits of solar energy.

While the four schools are geographically dispersed, their locations do not represent the whole range of American climatic conditions. So National Science Foundation scientists have contracted with Honeywell, Inc., to build and operate a mobile laboratory to tour the country.

One of the two trailers in the mobile lab is filled with solar-heating and -cooling test equipment plus a set of research weather instruments. The second trailer is a typical mobile home, except that it is heated and cooled by solar energy. The heat is collected by 650 square feet of panels outside the trailers. Under the winter sun, water circulating at eleven gal-

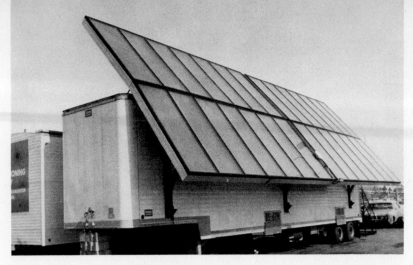

Honeywell's Transportable Solar Laboratory, sponsored by the Federal Energy Research and Development Administration, tours American cities to gather data for solar-energy conversion. Its objective is to aid architects and engineers in harnessing the sun's energy for heating and cooling buildings. *Honeywell, Inc.*

lons per minute can be heated to 130 degrees Fahrenheit. Part of that heat keeps the trailers warm during the day and supplies hot water; the rest is stored for use at night.

As the mobile lab tours the country, architects and building contractors will have a chance to see firsthand how solar-heating and -cooling systems work and how they can be applied to future construction. The mobile-home trailer will thus serve a double purpose as a mobile solar home and a roving classroom.

One American city that plans to "go solar" as soon as it can is Santa Clara, which lies about fifty miles south of San Francisco in a pleasant, sunny valley. As in many parts of California, rainfall is concentrated in the winter months, leaving nearly 300 days a year of clear skies. Until recently few people paid much attention to the possibilities of all that sunshine, but in mid-1975 Santa Clara completed a new recreation building that draws about 80 percent of its heating and cooling energy from solar collectors mounted on the roof. "What we see is a city-owned solar utility," said the city's manager. "We will finance and install solar-heating and -cooling systems in new buildings. Consumers will pay a monthly fee to cover amortization and maintenance of the solar units. This will be done on a nonprofit basis, with the capital raised from municipal bonds."

Dozens of corporations are presently involved in solar research, and some are already marketing solar-related products. And, judging from the millions of dollars it is pouring into solar research and development, the United States Government no longer dismisses the use of solar energy as farfetched. According to one study funded by the National Science Foundation, solar heating and cooling of buildings will be economically competitive in most parts of the United States by 1985–90, and these systems are presently almost competitive in sunny areas like Florida and California.

Only the area of solar electricity looks bleak—at least for the near future. If one could afford to buy photoelectric cells at several hundred dollars per square foot, it would be possible to run a house self-sufficiently on solar electricity. But to gen-

An engineer displays a new kind of solar-energy collector, a series of glass tubes, from which air has been removed, mounted in a module. Each tube contains an absorber plate through which a working fluid flows. *Corning Glass Works*

erate the amount of electricity and heating power used in a year, say 25,000 kilowatts, the roof would have to be covered with over 800 square feet of these photocells, at a cost that would run into tens of thousands of dollars. Even if these cells could be produced for as low as a dollar a square foot, as solar expert Karl Böer of the University of Delaware thinks they eventually can be, a solar-electric house would be prohibitively expensive. True, the day may come when buying electricity from the local power company costs more than making it at home with the sun's rays, but that day is not yet in sight. Nevertheless, useful and promising things are currently being done in the field of solar electricity.

CHAPTER FIVE

ELECTRICITY FROM THE SUN

Most of the energy we use today is electricity, a very safe and convenient form of power. We are also increasing our use of it about twice as fast as other forms, and eventually nearly all our energy requirements will be supplied by electricity. But its drawback is the very roundabout way it is produced. Fossil fuel of one kind or another is usually used to produce heat or steam, which in turn drives mechanical engines, which then actuate generators, which manufacture the electricity itself. However, electricity can be produced in a much more straight-forward fashion—directly from sunlight *without* using a solar collector.

We know that the solar radiation streaming down through the earth's atmosphere can generate useful heat, when it is absorbed and trapped, as in the thousands of solar hot-water heaters already installed in homes around the world. But heat is termed by scientists and engineers as "low-grade" energy compared with electricity, which can be transmitted long distances to power motors, computers, and indeed to give life to all the sophisticated machines required by modern technological nations. And the key to converting sunlight directly to high-grade electricity is the photovoltaic effect. (The term combines the Greek word *photo,* meaning *light,* and the name of Alessandro Volta, the Italian physicist, who pioneered in electricity.)

The photovoltaic effect can be defined as the generation of an electrical current by light falling upon the boundary between certain pairs of dissimilar materials. But what does this really mean?

Light is a form of energy. When light strikes certain chemical substances, such as selenium or silicon, its energy causes a push on the electrons in the substances. (An electron is part

Banks of solar cells absorb the sun's energy and convert it directly to electricity aboard an offshore oil platform in the Gulf of Mexico. The electricity is used for storage batteries that operate warning devices to alert passing ships to the position of the platform.

Continental Oil Company

of an atom; it spins in an orbit, or path, around the atom's nucleus, or center.) Such a push by the light energy can do one of three things to the electrons: 1) Sometimes it causes many of the electrons to break away from their atoms and become free electrons in the substance; 2) If the light has enough energy, some of the electrons can' jump completely out of the substance, leaving gaps in it, and into the surrounding space; 3) If two different substances happen to be touching one another, such as the silicon strips shown in the illustration, some of the electrons may leave one substance, leaving the same gaps, and enter the other.

Suppose now that an outside wire is attached to these substances to make a path for the electrons. As long as the light shines on the substances, a continuous flow of electrons takes place through the substances and the wire. Such a flow of electrons—in fact, any flow of electrons—is called an "electric current." A device that produces electric current when light shines on it is called a "photoelectric cell" or "photocell," or —in more modern engineering parlance because the photovoltaic effect is involved—a "photovoltaic cell." An electric current produced in this way is like any other electric current; it can be made to do work. It can also be stored in a battery for future use. When sunlight is used as the light source, the photovoltaic cell is sometimes called a "solar cell." If many solar cells are connected together, they make up what is called a "solar battery."

In modern photovoltaic cells, silicon is the substance often used to produce an electric current with sunlight. Silicon is a crystalline substance, and its atoms are built up in a latticelike framework, a situation in which the photovoltaic effect functions at its best. If an electron is jarred loose from a silicon atom by some outer force such as sunlight, it will wander freely through the crystal, leaving a gap, or hole, in the latticelike framework. This hole behaves like a positive charge of electricity. (Electrons are negatively charged particles and are attracted to, and flow toward, a positive source.) Every time an electron from an adjacent atom moves in to fill such a gap, it leaves a new gap behind it. In this way, holes can travel from one part of the crystal to another, just as the electrons can. When sunlight falls on the crystalline silicon, a certain number of freely wandering negative and positive charges are created within the crystal. They travel at random and tend to balance one another.

This balance must be upset, which is done by adding arsenic and boron to the silicon, if the photovoltaic effect is to produce current of any practical value. A typical silicon photovoltaic cell consists of two very thin strips, or wafers, of silicon. The strips are placed against each other. One strip, con-

opposite, top: A simple silicon photovoltaic cell. An electric current is set up as light strikes the cell and forces electrons to flow from the arsenic-silicon strip to the boron-silicon strip. Current can be measured with a galvanometer.

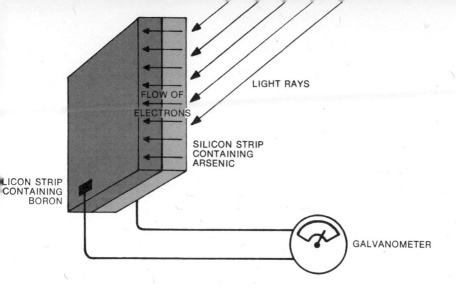

LIGHT RAYS

FLOW OF
ELECTRONS

SILICON STRIP
CONTAINING
ARSENIC

LICON STRIP
CONTAINING
BORON

GALVANOMETER

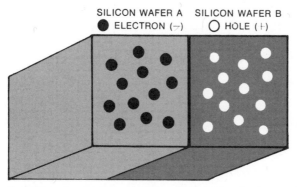

SILICON WAFER A   SILICON WAFER B
● ELECTRON (−)   ○ HOLE (+)

If a trace of arsenic is put into silicon wafer A, there will be
more electrons than holes. If boron is put into silicon wafer B,
there will be more holes than electrons.

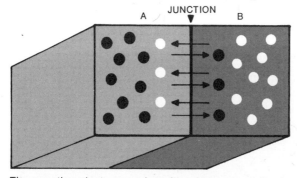

A   JUNCTION   B

The negative electrons and positive holes cross the junction
between wafers A and B. Wafer B will acquire a negative
charge as the electrons pass into it; A will acquire a positive
charge as it receives holes from B.

taining a tiny amount of arsenic, is called n-type silicon (*n* stands for negative), because the addition of the arsenic provides an excess of negative free electrons. The other strip, containing a tiny amount of boron, is called p-type silicon (*p* refers to its tendency to form positively charged holes). The boundary between the silicon-arsenic strip and the silicon-boron strip is called the "p-n junction." (In some processes, a single silicon wafer can be so treated and coated that it functions as a solar cell in itself.)

When sunlight strikes the cell, it knocks out electrons from the crystal lattice in the vicinity of the p-n junction and produces electron-hole pairs. Due to the presence of the positive holes and negative electrons on either side, a potential difference is established across the junction. Electrons are pulled across the junction one way and holes forced across in the opposite direction, thus forming an electric current. If terminals are built into each strip of silicon, a flow of electrons (the current) will stream from the negative terminal by way of electric wiring to the positive terminal. Current will flow in this way as long as sunlight strikes the silicon cell. Practical solar batteries consist of a number of such wafer cells set side by side and electrically connected.

Early solar batteries were round, the shape of wafers sawed from the crystalline ingot. Today most are rectangular and measure one by two centimeters and are about forty millimeters thick. A single photovoltaic cell of a typical battery weighs about two grams and develops an output in milliwatts (thousandths of a watt) at approximately half a volt in bright sunlight. Just as flashlight batteries are put together in series to give more power, solar batteries can be so connected to raise the voltage. Five cells can give about a two-volt rating, and twenty-eight-volt panels of connected cells are fairly common in space vehicles. Materials other than silicon, such as cadmium sulfide, have been used in the manufacture of cells.

The first photovoltaic cells with practical efficiencies were manufactured at Bell Laboratories in the early 1950's. By 1955, field tests had been conducted with small panels of cells mounted on the tops of telephone poles to power telephone amplifiers, or repeaters. Tried out on a modest scale at Amer-

In 1954, Bell Laboratories demonstrated the first practical solar cell. Here a lineman is shown installing a solar battery atop a telephone pole at Americus, Georgia. *Bell Telephone Laboratories*

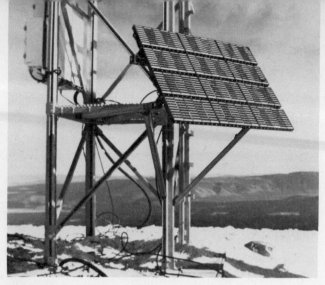

A Remote Automatic Meteorological Observation System weather station atop Mammoth Mountain, California, powered by silicon solar cells. _NASA_

icus, Georgia, the experiment worked quite well. The repeaters are needed at intervals in a telephone line to maintain and boost the strength of the signals transmitted. Since the power requirement for such repeaters is small, a solar battery could readily meet it. The Americus experiment typified the role played by solar cells over the past two decades, that of small, remote, specialty power sources.

One specialty power source very much in use today is RAMOS, an acronym for Remote Automatic Meteorological

opposite: A solar cell and its components. _inset:_ The cell used by missionaries in Peru to recharge radio-transmitter batteries with the sun's energy. _International Rectifier Corp._

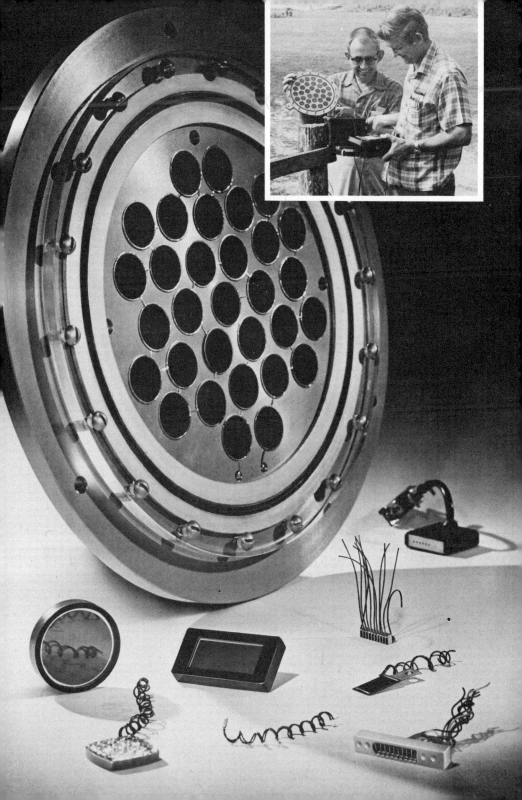

Observation System. RAMOS-type arrays of silicon solar cells are used primarily to power isolated weather stations, such as the one shown in the photograph. Using such solar cells saves refueling a weather station or replacing batteries. By 1985, the National Weather Service plans to have over 100 RAMOS stations that will form a meteorological network across the United States. Many will be in remote locations where weather conditions are hostile. In other specialty uses, solar cells are often employed to recharge radio-transmitter batteries at remote outposts, such as Antarctica. One was used recently for this purpose by missionaries in Peru.

By far the most successful use of solar cells today is in space. They have been installed in several thousand satellites launched since 1958. The reasons for their success are obvious. In space (above the atmosphere) sunlight strikes the solar cells continuously so that there is no lack of light needed for the photovoltaic effect to take place on silicon surfaces. Also, the power requirements for the satellites are low, which solar cells can amply and constantly provide. Finally, keeping in mind the high cost of solar cells, expense is no barrier to nations with active space programs.

The solar batteries are usually arranged on flat plates along the outside of the spacecraft or on huge, flat paddles, or arrays, attached to the sides of the craft. When the sun shines on the batteries, they generate an electric current sufficient to charge storage batteries inside the spacecraft and to operate

Explorer satellites like this one, launched in the 1960's, were equipped with over 5000 solar cells. *U.S. Air Force*

various instruments, such as camera motors, aboard the craft.

The Explorer series of satellites launched in the early 1960's had over 5000 solar cells, capable of delivering five watts of power. And Bell System's fabulously successful series of Telstar communications satellites, used to boost and relay radio and TV signals from one place on earth to another, had some 3600 cells in all. The Telstars are roughly spherical in shape with dozen of facets on their outside. Solar cells are mounted on most of these facets on ceramic bases in platinum frames; coverings of clear man-made sapphire protect them from bombardment by charged particles and meteoroids in space. The

Attaching solar cells and transparent sapphire slices to a Telstar satellite. Solar cells are covered with the sapphire to protect them from space radiation. *Bell Telephone Laboratories*

Telstar solar cells convert sunlight into electric current that charges about twenty nickel-cadmium cells, which in turn provide power for the electronic circuits in the satellite.

Solar cells have proved their indispensability in space year after year. By 1965, the National Aeronautics and Space Administration (NASA) was using close to a million a year. In the United States space program, a few of the spacecraft employing solar-battery arrays are: the first tiny Vanguard satellites; the Tiros and Nimbus weather satellites; the Telstar, Early Bird, and Syncom communications satellites; the Luna

Orbiter that surveyed the moon; the Orbiting Astronomical Observatory (OAO); the Mariner series of spacecraft whose flybys radioed back important information about Mars and Venus; and the Pioneer series that surveyed Jupiter, Saturn, and other outer planets of the solar system. Many of these satellites and spacecraft are still in orbit or in flight, with their solar cells functioning as well as ever.

Skylab, America's first manned space station, carries the largest solar-array system ever flown. Built by TRW Systems, Inc., for NASA, the system has dual 28- by 30-foot wings, each of which contains 1147 square feet of energy-conversion

Solar cells installed on the four paddles of an S-3 satellite.
Bell Telephone Laboratories

Technicians check one of Skylab's foldable solar-array wings before installation in the spacecraft. *TRW Systems, Inc.*

surface to supply primary electric power to the orbital work-shop where the astronauts carry out scientific work. The two solar-array wings produce 12,240 watts minimum power at fifty-five volts. Each wing contains 147,840 king-size solar cells and is formed in three sections that can be folded back accordion fashion and deployed again within four minutes. During the Skylab missions conducted in 1973 and 1974, there was initial trouble when one of the wings would not deploy properly, thus cutting down on the power essential for the astronauts to perform their work successfully. However, the trouble was adjusted, and each of the three-man crews went on to conduct invaluable scientific investigations in space. Skylab was the first manned space vehicle to rely almost completely on the sun for electricity, and its work could not have been carried out without the utilization of solar energy.

Obviously the silicon photovoltaic solar cell is a successful

Skylab 4 in orbit over the cloud-covered earth. Note the missing solar panel on left, which was lost on launch day. *NASA*

Using this new method of crystal growing in which single-crystal silicon strips are drawn continuously from a crucible, photovoltaic conversion of electricity may soon have cheaper, longer-lived solar cells.

National Science Foundation

invention, but still it has had no significant impact—except in space—on world energy consumption to date. This situation seems strange, since almost all solar cells are made from silicon, which is the second most abundant element in the earth's crust. Moreover, silicon of metellurgical purity that is used in making solar cells costs only about $600 per ton. Why, then, do solar cells sell for about $50,000 per electrical kilowatt (about $50 per watt), roughly 500 times too high for successful competition with fossil fuel and nuclear power plants? The reason is painfully obvious when one considers the long and wasteful process by which they are manufactured today.

The common silicon solar cell is made from an artificially grown crystal. The basic technique for growing such crystals was developed by an inventor named Czochralski, whose method of "pulling" a crystal from a batch of silicon melt is tedious, expensive, and requires many highly trained (and highly paid) workers. The Czochralski method also requires precise temperature control and skilled operators who know exactly when to add the raw silicon to the batch lest it crystallize too fast. Further steps in the process involve the slow sawing and polishing of the thin wafers. (Much of the carefully nurtured crystal ends up as powder on the floor, rather than solar cells.) Next, the circular wafers must be cut into squares and rectangles (another wasteful step) and then sent to the ovens to diffuse the impurities. Finally, electrical connections must be laboriously added and the finished cells mounted to create large arrays.

As some solar scientists complain about the so-called Czochralskian dilemma, "There must be a better way." The National Science Foundation would like to bring down solar-cell costs to about fifty cents per watt, or about five hundred dollars per installed kilowatt, which would make them almost competitive with existing power plants. Presently the National Science Foundation is supporting a number of newer and cheaper ways of making reliable, long-lived solar cells. However, the fact remains that no one has really tried very hard to make cheap solar cells because no large market for

A thermoelectric converter built by General Electric in Arizona.

General Electric Co.

them has existed. But today the growing pressure for alternate power sources makes it worthwhile to explore some of these cheaper and less wasteful manufacturing possibilities.

Although the photovoltaic cell is the simplest and most direct way to convert sunlight to electric power, it is not the only direct conversion method. Thermoelectric conversion can change the sun's *heat* into electric current. Actually the method was discovered as early as 1822 by the German physicist Thomas Johann Seebeck while experimenting with heat and magnetism in various metals. Seebeck found that when heat is applied to a junction between two metals, an electric current will flow. Formerly called the "Seebeck effect," the phenomenon is more commonly known today as the "photoelectric effect." A modern application is the thermostat that regulates the turning on and off of furnaces by means of a thermocouple.

A thermocouple is a device made of two different metals joined at an angle. An electric current is generated when the joint, or junction, becomes hotter than the other parts of the metal. In solar applications, the heat is produced by focusing the sun's rays, usually by means of a mirror collector. In the thermoelectric converter, such a collector focuses sunlight onto thermocouples only a few inches in diameter. Although thermoelectric generators for powering radios and other equipment in outlying areas and some thermoelectric refrigerators have been produced, efficiencies are low and the cost of reflector mirrors is high. Nevertheless, a big advantage of thermoelectricity over the solar battery is that many firms today are working with thermoelectric materials but only a few are producing solar batteries. Also, nearly any heat source will operate a thermoelectric junction, but the same is not true for photovoltaic cells.

Other methods have also been used to change solar energy directly into electricity. However, they have been largely experimental and at present too costly to develop for widespread commercial use. One of them is called "thermoionic conversion" and involves the emission of electrons inside an electronic vacuum tube. When heat in the form of sunlight is applied to the cathode (negative) electrode in the vacuum tube, electrons are made to flow from it toward the anode (positive) electrode, thus generating an electric current. A handful of fairly successful thermoionic converters have been built, notably for the United States Air Force, but so demanding is the technology involved that solar experts think it will be years before they can be produced at a competitive cost.

Thus far only a few token attempts have been made to use electricity produced directly from the sun to supplement conventional energy sources on earth. France, the country with the largest solar furnace, also has built the largest thermo-electric generator, located near Toulon. However, it is only a prototype for test purposes to pave the way for a much larger 700-square-foot generator. In the United States, Radio Corporation of America engineers have designed and tested

The Baker electric car, called the world's first sun-powered automobile, is powered by a large solar panel on the roof.

International Rectifier Corp.

thermoelectric converters using metal reflectors to focus the sun's rays and produce small amounts of power in rural areas. Westinghouse is also developing such thermoelectric converters. The small-scale power plants can pump water and furnish electricity for lighting and communication, refrigeration, and other uses. And General Electric is experimenting with thermoionic converters to generate power for similar purposes.

Thus, considering the success it has had in the space field, photovoltaic power seems to hold a promising future for man in creating electricity directly from sunlight. Nevertheless, many practical-minded engineers have their doubts that solar cells—even if their cost could be sufficiently lowered—can be of much future value in any but specialty markets. They point to the publicity that has been given to such sun-powered gadgets as solar radios, fans, toy airplanes and boats, shavers, flashlights, and even cars that run on sunlight. "Once a toy," they say, "always a toy."

Yet the scientific principles upon which solar cells operate remain sound, costs of materials and methods are being shaved, and public confidence in the practicality of solar energy itself is on the upswing. Projects like Skylab and Solar One are steps in the right direction, but eventually something more impressive in scope must be tried whereby entire cities can be powered and thousands of homes heated by the sun. Some imaginative solar-minded thinkers have already planned and designed such impressive projects.

CHAPTER SIX

THE FUTURE

A number of daring and imaginative ideas concerning the future use of the sun in our lives have been proposed. Some have been labeled as too futuristic, others as out-and-out fantasy. A few have been thought out to the last economic and technical detail. But in a world that is increasingly hard put to find new sources of energy, political leaders are presently taking a closer look at a number of these solar-energy schemes.

The most promising are receiving more than casual scrutiny today, especially by American solar scientists. Here is a description of them under their project names:

Solar Farms and a National Solar Power Facility

The use of large areas of cheap land to collect or farm sufficient quantities of solar energy to run electrical-power installations has often been proposed as a plausible alternative to conventional energy sources. The basic idea of a solar farm is to set up on vast tracts of unusable land—probably in desert areas where the sun shines most of the year—array after array of either flat-plate collectors or solar-battery panels. If flat-plate collectors are used, the heat harvested can be turned into steam, which can drive turbines, which in turn can produce electric power. If photovoltaics are used, electricity is harvested directly. Both types of farms have the twin advantages of being low in cost to maintain and relatively free of pollution. Moreover, advocates of solar farms say that crops could be grown beneath the warm panels or that cattle could graze underneath them and use them for shelter.

Among the serious proponents of solar farms using photovoltaic batteries is William R. Cherry, long a NASA scientist working to develop power systems for space craft. In 1971, Cherry predicted, "A pollution-free method of converting

Solar-energy farms of the future may generate electricity by harvesting sunshine. In this artist's concept, heat-absorbing panels collect energy to be distributed. Note flow of working fluid in the panels as they are heated. *University of Arizona, artist Don Cowen*

solar energy directly into electric power using photovoltaics on the ground shows that sunlight falling on about 1 percent of the land area of the forty-eight states could provide the total electrical power requirements of the United States in the year 1990."

Cherry has suggested a modest start could be made by setting up a solar-energy farm of one square mile, which could be built on otherwise useless land. The electricity harvested on such a farm could provide electric current for some 18,000 homes. However, to supply the entire United States by 1990 would require solar farms covering approximately 31,-500 square miles, or 1 percent of the continental United States.

Obviously Cherry's proposal depends upon a dramatic reduction in the cost of photovoltaic cells. Indeed, the practical electrical engineers who presently must manufacture these cells by tedious and wasteful methods tend to snort with disbelief when they hear talk of covering Arizona deserts with square miles of precious silicon wafers. Yet ultimately, Cherry suggests, costs might go as low as fifty dollars a kilowatt and, with mechanized factory production, a solar blanket of large size could be produced. In fact, one or two firms are already talking of developing a way of producing mile-long silicon crystals in the form of ribbons as thin as human hair. When and if such techniques result in the mass production of cheap solar batteries, William Cherry's vision of an economical and long-lasting photovoltaic farm would be well worth the trouble and cost of building. For once built, nothing can match the simple efficiency and elegance of the solar battery that just sits in the sun and changes light into electric current.

Another plan has been developed by the husband-and-wife team of Aden and Marjorie Meinel of the University of Arizona. They claim that they would need only 5000 instead of 31,500 square miles to do the same job with a more highly

Solar scientists Marjorie and Aden Meinel inspect a new test model of a parabolic cylindrical solar collector. *University of Arizona*

efficient conversion process involving flat-plate collectors. Being practical and realistic scientists, the Meinels call their proposed power plant the National Solar Power Facility, and they have planned it down to the last detail.

Basically their facility would be built in units, each capable of supplying 1000 megawatts. If completed according to plan, it would produce 1 billion kilowatts of solar electricity, sufficient power to serve the needs of the entire United States. The 5000-square-mile collection area would be located in uninhabited desert acreage in Arizona, California, and Nevada, where the first of the 1000 megawatt plants would be built. The entire facility, the Meinels estimate, would take a century to complete.

The Meinels' solar energy plant is fundamentally simple in design. Heat from the sun is collected by array after array of flat-plate collectors. Those collectors would be tipped or otherwise adjusted to the proper sun angle from time to time for greater efficiency. The heat produced would then be piped away from the banks of collectors by a working fluid to the central plant, where it would generate steam. The steam

opposite, top: The Meinel's model of the solar-energy farm using medium temperature flat-plate collectors with selective surfaces to increase temperature efficiency. The power plant is located in the center of the four quadrants. *bottom:* A close-up of the central power plant showing rows of flat-plate collectors. *University of Arizona*

would then be used to drive a conventional steam-turbine generator, which in turn manufactures electricity.

The Meinels claim that the solar-thermal-conversion system they propose can operate at temperatures as high as 1000 degrees Fahrenheit. As we have seen, the traditional method of achieving such high temperatures to make steam uses mirrors, reflectors, or lenses to focus the sun's rays. However, the Meinels have come up with two innovations that will substantially boost their operating temperature. One is the use of a specially prepared selective surface or solar black coating for the collectors, which absorbs most of the solar heat and loses very little of it. The second involves the use of a new working fluid. Instead of piping away the solar heat in water, as most systems do, the Meinels plan to circulate liquid sodium containing a mixture of molten salts between the glass collectors and the main storage tank. The liquid sodium, which is capable of retaining more heat than ordinary water, would transfer this heat to the storage tank, which acts as a heat reservoir to operate the turbines. The plant would also be designed to keep the turbines operating at acceptable efficiencies overnight and during other periods of lowered solar radiation.

An adequate water supply could be a big stumbling block to the Meinels' proposed facility. To make steam, a steam-turbine-electric plant needs water, and the Southwestern American desert region is arid. Their solution is to bring in seawater in huge aqueducts from the Pacific Ocean and the

Gulf of California to provide the steam. Though construction and pumping costs will be high, they would be largely offset by the fresh water that the solar plant would yield as a by-product. A supply of cheap fresh water would stimulate farming in these present-day wastelands and make them fit for settlement, as would the cheap electricity provided by the plant itself.

Although a number of other problems would also have to be dealt with, the National Solar Power Facility has been described as the most thoroughly researched and documented solar-energy project ever proposed. In recent years, the Meinels have been traveling about the country explaining their facility to everyone who will listen and trying to get financial support for it. Already they have stimulated enough interest to obtain several thousands of dollars in grants and aids from the National Science Foundation and other organizations. The Meinels hope first to be able to begin work on a small pilot plant to demonstrate the feasibility of the entire facility. Next, the first of the 1000 megawatt plants could be completed sometime in the 1980's. If it proves to be useful technically and economically, work could begin on several other plants in the proposed complex. Indeed, if the Meinels' dream is finally fulfilled in the decades ahead, the great-grandchildren of Americans living today will be getting all the electricity they need from the National Solar Power Facility.

Solar Satellite Power Stations

Just as some scientists envision large ground-based solar plants, so others see giant solar-energy collectors orbiting the earth in the black, airless emptiness of space. The advantages of such a collection system are obvious. In space, there is stronger and steadier radiation on which to draw; there are no clouds or other obstructions to cut down reception of sunlight; and if more than one satellite is used, solar energy can be collected twenty-four hours a day. The notion of such an orbiting solar power station, the object of which is to mass-produce electricity for use on earth, is not new. Indeed, it has intrigued solar scientists for quite a few years.

One scientist, Peter E. Glaser of Arthur D. Little, Inc., has done more than just dream about such a project. Like the Meinels, he has also planned out in great detail what he calls the Solar Satellite Power Station, or SSPS. In addition to the advantages already mentioned, Glaser sees others in the system he contemplates. In space, there would be no wind to disturb the huge structure that would house the collectors. Further, the conversion method would be by long-lived solar batteries that require little or no maintenance. Also, by correctly orienting the solar satellite in space to face the sun, it would receive the sun's rays directly rather than at an angle. Finally, Glaser has proposed that two such satellites could be used spaced about 8000 miles apart in their orbit. This arrangement would prevent loss of sunlight to the system when one of the two satellites is hidden from the sun by the earth's shadow. Or a network of more than two satellites could be put into orbit to serve more than one ground station.

The colossal size of Glaser's SSPS challenges the imagination. Basically, as seen in the accompanying photograph, there would be two huge collectors containing solar-cell panels, each having an area of sixteen square kilometers (or about six and a quarter square miles). Each of these

A model of the proposed Satellite Solar Power Station that would produce 10,000 megawatts of electric power.

NASA; art courtesy of Grumman Corp.

gigantic collectors would face the sun and look like an open box because of mirror concentrators attached to the four sides. The two collectors would be joined together, and at the center of the whole complex would be a transmitting antenna of one square kilometer. This antenna would point directly at a receiving antenna on earth with a diameter of seven kilometers. The SSPS would be able to generate 10,000 megawatts of electricity (1 megawatt equals 1 million watts), enough to power a good-sized city. But such a power station is only a pilot model; if Peter Glaser could have his way, a much larger one would be built.

How, one might well ask at this point, does a huge contraption way out in space transfer the electrical energy it has collected back to earth without wires or cables? The plan is that each of the huge collectors, consisting of many hundreds of solar-battery panels connected together, gathers its electric power and transmits it some two miles via large cables to the central transmitting antenna. There it is beamed to the earth through some 22,000 miles of space. First, however, it must be converted from the direct electrical energy made by the photovoltaics to a more beamable

opposite: Artists' concepts of different forms that a solar power plant could take. Currently under study by several companies, both would use the basic idea of transmitting solar energy back to earth in the form of microwaves. *Arthur D. Little, Inc.; NASA*

kind of energy. The kind that scientists like Glaser think will work best is microwave radiation, more commonly known as radar. Scientists already know a great deal about handling radar and how these microwaves can be pointed accurately and transmitted.

A portion of the solar-power-plant space would consist of special amplifiers that would generate the microwave radiation. The proposed transmitting antenna, aimed at the receiver on earth, would be in the shape of a dish about one kilometer in diameter. Pointing the transmitter precisely so that it keeps "locked on" continually to the earth station will require advanced techniques, but engineers and scientists think they can solve this problem when the time comes.

When the incoming microwave radiation reaches the earth, it will be absorbed by a large array of rectifiers and converted again into direct-current electricity at a very high efficiency. For practical use on earth, this direct current would then be reconverted into alternating current, the kind we use in our homes and industrial complexes. The power would be fed into regular grid distribution networks, using special conductor cables to minimize current loss, so that it can be passed along to private and industrial consumers of electricity.

Obviously a project the size of the SSPS poses a number of technical problems, not the least of which is how to get a structure consisting of square *miles* of equipment into space

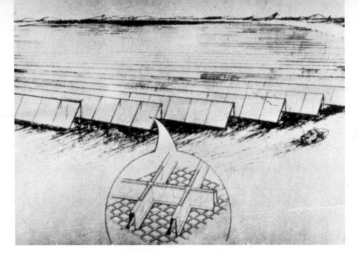

Incoming microwave radiation from solar power plants would be received by large arrays such as this, then converted to conventional electricity.   *Arthur D. Little, Inc.*

orbit. Piece by manageable piece of the whole would have to be transferred out to space and assembled there. Glaser and others point out that the space shuttle, due to be operational in the 1980's, could be used for this task, with space "tugs" moving individual modules and payloads for assembly in a low-earth orbit. As to the practicality of space-borne assemblies of such huge size and weight—estimates run to about five million pounds for the SSPS—Glaser and other scientists indicate that larger projects have been studied for use in space. For example, gigantic radio telescopes have been designed by astronomers to be assembled in earth orbit. Some of them even exceed the size of the solar collectors that would be used for the SSPS.

Quite apart from its enormous cost, there are objections to a

Artist's concept of a large space station with a solar power plant being assembled in space. Note space tugs towing parts out to the rendezvous area. *NASA, artist Frank Tinsley*

solar satellite power plant on humanitarian grounds. Some critics say that the concentrated microwaves being beamed to earth would act as a "death ray" that would destroy anything in its way. Glaser admits that if the power concentration of the microwave beam is nearly one watt per square centimeter, it would be greater than normal sunlight and could conceivably harm human skin or other objects that might enter the beam. Even so, the beam would not be strong enough to burn houses or melt aircraft that flew in its way. The solution, Glaser suggests, would be to reduce the strength of the beam substantially, while increasing the size of the microwave receiver on earth.

Other critics ask why such an orbiting solar plant should be put into space at all. Although the concentrated microwave energy reaching the earth would provide more power than ordinary sunlight, couldn't the same amount be produced by building an extra-large collection system on the ground? Glaser and others reply no. As it passes through the atmosphere, sunlight is weakened by water vapor and other impurities, which does not happen with microwave radiation. This radar energy, beamed straight at the earth from the SSPS, would lose very little of its strength to the atmosphere, leaving more for man's use. Also, a large ground-based collector would always have the nighttime factor and cloudy days to cut down its efficiency, while the SSPS would be almost always in perpetual sunlight.

In February, 1972, Glaser and a team of other scientists presented testimony for a proposed SSPS of 10,000 megawatts before the Committee on Science and Astronautics of the United States House of Representatives. One by one the various scientists of the study team testified to the feasibility *today* of undertaking this imaginative project. The price tag to the United States Government would be several billions, but so was the twenty-billion-dollar gamble to reach the moon. If in the future this multibillion-dollar step is taken successfully, the rewards in abundant and pollution-free electrical energy will be great indeed.

Ocean-Thermal-Difference Power Plants

By far the largest collector of solar energy is the vast surface area of the world's oceans and seas. Since the tropical regions of the globe consist largely of ocean, most of the sunlight falling on the earth is absorbed and stored up in these waters. At the surface their temperature is 82 to 85 degrees Fahrenheit. Yet they are separated by as little as 2000 feet from a virtually inexhaustible cold-water reservoir with temperatures of 35 to 38 degrees.

These near-freezing, dense waters have traveled from the polar regions, where they slide under the warmer and more bouyant surface waters moving poleward. The two water layers keep separated, and the thermal (heat) difference between them can be used by man to produce energy.

In marked contrast to solar-power systems employing artificial collectors, the ocean thermal difference is a constant source of energy. Thermal-energy storage reservoirs, such as large insulated water tanks, aren't necessary because the ocean itself is the reservoir. Tapping the potential energy between the hot and cold layers of water depends upon whether practical energy-conversion equipment can operate on the temperature difference of 50 degrees. This small temperature variation is roughly the difference between the inside and outside of a home refrigerator. In contrast, a coal-fired power plant commonly operates at differences of 800 degrees Fahrenheit. Yet low-efficiency heat engines exist that can run on these small temperature differences, and it has been estimated that, employing such engines, the Gulf Stream alone could provide seventy-five times the energy needs of the entire United States.

Such a modern heat-transfer system that would work at sea is based on the principle that a difference in temperature can be employed to produce mechanical energy. An electricity-generating turbine can be turned by the force of some working fluid, such as propane or ammonia, which becomes a gas and expands when suddenly warmed by tropical surface water. Afterward the gas is condensed back to its fluid state by the cooler water pumped up from the depths of the ocean floor and used again and again in the cycle. In the past, water was used as the working fluid, but it is an inefficient substance.

The ocean-thermal-difference idea is almost a hundred years old, having first been conceived by the French physicist Jacques Arsene d'Arsonval in the 1880's. But its real pioneer was another distinguished French scientist, Georges Claude of Paris. Claude began his experiments in ocean thermal energy in 1926 by successfully operating, in his laboratory, a small turbine that generated sixty kilowatts of power, using a temperature difference of only about 35 degrees Fahrenheit.

But Claude was determined to build a plant that would operate under actual sea conditions. Eventually he chose a location in the tropical waters off Cuba, where he and the crew members of his expedition spent long, backbreaking months trying to moor a gigantic steel pipe to the ocean floor. The pipe was six feet in diameter and over a mile long, and Claude watched two of them sink to the bottom before he succeeded in securing a third properly.

Harassed by hurricanes, poor work by near-mutinous crews, and a host of other problems, Claude finally got his ocean thermal plant working. Using a temperature difference of only about 27 degrees Fahrenheit, he succeeded in developing 22 kilowatts of power with his test engine. Some of Claude's critics scornfully pointed out that he was using more power to pump the cold water up from the depths than he produced at the ocean surface. Yet he was so sure that he was on the right track that he began making plans to build a new plant off Santiago de Cuba that would produce 25,000 kilowatts.

Though the plant was never built, Claude refused to give up his dream of harvesting energy from the sea. This time, chartering the old steamer *Tunisie,* he suspended a lengthy cold-water pipe beneath the vessel, thus making a floating thermal plant that worked quite well. Already in his sixties, Claude courageously continued his expensive experiments into the mid-1930's, but died at the age of ninety without having seen any really productive results in the field of thermal ocean energy.

Sporadic attempts have been made by others to reap the harvest of energy stored in the sea. The French Government, hoping to carry on Claude's work, experimented in 1950 off the Ivory Coast of Africa, envisioning a floating thermal plant. In the United States, Asa Snyder, of the Pratt and Whitney Company, proposed in 1961 a modest 5000 kilowatt sea-thermal power plant on land with a cold-water intake pipe slanting into the nearby ocean and continuing down into a submarine canyon. Although the basic design is the same as Claude's, Snyder thinks that with today's improved technology his plant could operate with far greater efficiency. One innovation in Snyder's design would be to heat the surface water with a solar heater, a method that was not very successful for Claude and his colleagues.

A larger and more concrete proposal for an ocean thermal plant has been made by two mechanical engineers in California, Hilbert Anderson and James Anderson. The Andersons' plant would be a large, free-floating bargelike structure, capable of producing 100 megawatts of electric power, which could move from one location to another in the ocean.

It would be 360 feet long with a central cold-water pipe 40 feet in diameter and 2000 feet long, suspended straight down into the ocean. Such a free-floating thermal plant could be moved to find warmer water, and it would not need as long a cold-water pipe to reach the necessary depth as a land-based plant whose pipe slants out to the ocean bottom. With its boilers and other equipment designed to rest below the water's surface, the Andersons' floating plant would be extremely stable and suffer no damage from heavy storms at sea.

The Andersons' floating plant differs radically from Claude's pioneering efforts in its use of propane as the working medium. Propane is not only cheap and readily available, but the propane turbine is smaller and cheaper to manufacture than a conventional steam turbine. In operation, the warm surface water would be taken in through screens that sift out unwanted material, then pumped through the boilers to vaporize the propane working fluid. The heated propane then turns the turbine to manufacture electric current. Afterward the propane goes to a condenser, where it is reliquefied by the cold water pumped up from the ocean depths.

In any floating thermal plant, the problem remains of how to get the electric power ashore to consumers, for a bargelike structure such as the Andersons' may often be operating several miles out to sea. Probably submarine cables—heavily insulated wiring laid on the sea bottom—could do the job. However, using microwave wireless transmission of the power, as Glaser proposes in his solar-orbiting satellite, might also be feasible.

Advocates of ocean-thermal-difference plants also like to point to other advantages of their system besides the obvious one of manufacturing electric power. One is the production of valuable by-products. In the Andersons' system—and a similar one, designed to be built completely submerged, that the National Science Foundation is investigating—the propane cycle used desalinates millions of gallons of fresh water to points where it could be used ashore. Other by-products of thermal energy from the sea are oxygen, salt, and several minerals. Steel plants, for example, require vast quantities of power, oxygen, and fresh water, which an ocean thermal plant would produce.

Finally, scientists think it very likely that these large floating plants would enhance the commercial-fishing prospects in the areas where they are moored. Marine biologists have long known that cold, nutrient-rich water welling up from the ocean bottom results in fertile fishing grounds. Not only would the thermal plant bring up the cold water, it would keep it heated at the surface where the fish feed, and fishermen could catch them in large numbers.

The concept of solar sea power is obviously still in the visionary stage, but pioneers like Georges Claude have pre-

111

Artist's concept of a largely submerged ocean-thermal power plant that would operate on the temperature differences between warm surface water and frigid deep water.   *National Science Foundation*

sented ample evidence that it will work. The technology exists today to build these floating power plants; no new technical breakthroughs are necessary. Meanwhile, until governments of the world are willing to finance them, the sea waits—the greatest reservoir on our planet of stored solar energy.

Wind Power

The great weather systems that wheel across the world's continents are actually sun-driven atmospheric machines that generate more power, if tapped, than all fossil-fuel power plants put together. Solar heat circulates the atmosphere; hence wind-driven machines must be considered a form of solar energy. To the pioneers on the windswept Great Plains of the United States, the windmill was a good source of power. For a period of fifty years more than six million windmills pumped water, sawed wood, and generated electric power in the American West. Today few windmills remain, for the rural electrification programs of the 1930's made them obsolete.

This situation may well change in the future. Some power engineers now foresee wind-power generators once more strung across the Plains, perhaps numbering in the thousands, replacing or augmenting fossil-fuel power plants. Others speculate on batteries of windmills anchored off the United States East Coast, taking advantage of dependable offshore winds. The picturesque prairie windmills will never return, but in their stead will be large-scale, sleek, new wind generators built from modern materials, serving the nation's power grid rather than isolated homesteads.

Abundant wind power, like sunshine, is there for the taking. It has been estimated that practical wind-driven power plants could generate as much as one trillion kilowatt-hours annually—more than half of the annual consumption in the United States. This energy resource was not economical as long as fossil fuels were cheap. Now the use of wind power will compare more favorably, depending on the progress made in several technical areas.

On some parts of the Great Plains, or even in cities like Chicago, the Windy City, the wind seems to blow incessantly. But wind is really not that constant. It veers and gusts and may even disappear for days on end. More than any other kind of power-generating technique, wind power is dogged by inconstancy and fickleness. These lags and variations in the wind have a big effect on the power that a windmill generating electricity will put out.

If a gusty wind is driving a conventional alternating-current generator, the frequency of the current (the number of cycles of current per second), which is related to how fast the windmill's shaft is turning, will fluctuate wildly. For an electrical power system finely tuned to a constant sixty-cycle current—the rate ordinarily used in homes—these fluctuations cannot be tolerated. One solution would be to feed the fluctuating power into a reservoir that is insensitive to frequency variations; for example, rectifiers could convert it to direct current, which is noncyclical, steadily flowing current. Engineers are also investigating other promising solutions to the problem.

The variability of the wind also makes it hard to know

just how much power can be generated at a particular site and what kind of equipment would be most efficient to use. To build an effective, reliable wind-power plant, the wind's velocity must be known as exactly as possible. Moreover, it must be known at particular altitudes (winds are "jumpier" closer to the ground, because of obstructions on the earth, than they are higher up). In short, engineers must

Harnessing wind energy created by the sun. A model of the 100-kilowatt windmill soon to go into service on the shores of Lake Erie.

NASA

have more information about wind behavior than is available now. One of the National Science Foundation's highest priorities is to gain this knowledge so that the best sites can be selected for new wind-power turbines.

Despite these obstacles, wind power demands no major technological breakthroughs. Systems could be built immediately. In fact, one was built as early as 1940 and used successfully in Vermont to generate 1.25 megawatts of power. It was finally shut down because of fatigue failures in the rotor, not because of the inconstancy or failure of the wind.

Today, at the National Aeronautics and Space Administration's Lewis Research Center in Cleveland, Ohio, a 100-kilowatt windmill is being built and will soon go into operation on the windy shores of Lake Erie. A forerunner of much

The Vertical Axis Windmill at Langley Research Center, Virginia, can convert wind power to electricity on a small scale.   *NASA*

larger systems that could supply between 5 and 10 percent of the country's power needs by the year 2000, the windmill is being developed as a part of the United States' solar-energy program. This experimental windmill will have a tower 125 feet tall and rotor blades measuring 125 feet from tip to tip. The horizontal cylinder at the top will contain the power transmission and control systems. Later NASA will supply to the Government of Puerto Rico a similar wind-power generator that will service many homes with electricity.

Presently NASA is testing a device called a Vertical Axis Windmill (VAW) at Langley Research Center in Virginia that will convert wind power to electricity for individual houses on a small smale. As can be seen in the photograph, its airfoil (wing-shaped) blades can rotate in almost any wind situation to provide energy to power a typical single-family house. One small American company is already offering wind-power equipment for homes. Eventually many homes could have their own wind turbines to produce electricity and perhaps to drive wind furnaces for heating as well.

Bioconversion

For 80 million years under the power of the sun, the coal swamps grew, and died, and grew, and died, and built up rich layers of hydrocarbons. For another 340 million years, after sediments covered this hydrocarbon debris, the pressures of the earth squeezed the swamp crops dry and condensed them into the black energy we call coal.

Scientists point out that there is nothing in the coal that wasn't in the swamp plants, so why not, in our present energy crisis, short circuit those 340 million years of geological time by growing our own crops and treating them for use as if they were a kind of low-grade coal? The essential hydrocarbons are present in today's plants just as they were in those of the Carboniferous period, and a variety of laboratory proceses can convert them into familiar fuel forms.

The process by which it is possible to grow crops—which are a basic result of sunlight falling on our planet—specifically for burning to produce power is known as bioconversion. Trees, grasses, algae, and other plants all capture and store solar energy. These materials can, of course, be burned directly for heat, but by putting them through various chemical processes, they can be converted, or up-graded, into high-grade fuels.

Some of the plant products that can be bioconverted into higher-grade fuels include trees, sugarcane, marine plants, and a host of others. One method is to heat the material in a vacuum to make gas and oil, thereby cutting a few million years off nature's timetable for doing the same job. The method is "pyrolysis" and a few manufacturing plants using it have already operated successfully. Through a fermentation process, watery mixtures of organic matter have been converted to methane, or natural, gas and various useful chemicals. Dried organic wastes can also be converted to burnable oil at high temperatures in a vacuum.

In bioconversion, the foremost problem is to collect enough biomass—the organic vegetation to be converted—cheaply enough to be competitive with other energy sources. Already some scientists envision huge "energy plantations" where plants such as sunflowers, sorghums, eucalyptus, and water hyacinth, which have high potential as biomass, can be grown. On these plantations the energy from the sun, instead of heating water or activating photovoltaics, would simply do what it has been doing for eons—making plants grow. These plants could then be harvested for biomass and bioconverted as usable fuels.

Quite apart from future energy plantations, there already exist great quantities of what might be considered harvested, collected, and even partly digested biomass—the organic portion of trash, garbage, and sewage. This solid waste is presently a great worry to city managers as they try to dispose of it without polluting the air, rivers, or countryside. A city the size of Holyoke, Massachusetts, for example, with a population of 50,000, could convert its own solid waste into a third of a billion cubic feet of clean-burning methane gas—about 13 percent of the area's usage.

It seems likely that economically viable bioconversion systems will be developed in the near future. Two major investigations with National Science Foundation support are already underway, one on the East Coast and another in the Midwest. Other allied investigations are being supported by the Environmental Protection Agency. According to National Science Foundation estimates, an accelerated bioconversion program might be providing as much as 8 percent of United States' energy needs by the year 2000.

Solar Energy Storage and a Hydrogen Economy

Ground-based solar-thermal power plants, photovoltaic power plants, wind-power plants, and ocean thermal plants are all essentially different from fossil-fuel electric plants. The solar units using sunshine streaming through the atmosphere can operate only during clear weather and daylight hours, and the wind units only when breezes blow. Unlike fossil-fuel plants, which can be set up almost anywhere if need be, these plants are restricted to special locations, such as sun-drenched areas, windy regions, and offshore sites.

Thus the problem arises of how solar-made electric power, produced in remote areas, can be integrated into widespread power grid systems like those in the United States. One Government study has revealed that solar power could not contribute more than about 20 percent of the country's total electricity requirements unless new ways are found to store transportable energy for later use. Those who conducted the study reason that right now almost 75 percent of the United States' electrical power consumption falls in the base-load category; that is, the power is needed all the time, night and day, in sunny and cloudy weather. Solar energy cannot provide the base load with a way to store the power it generates during the day, although it can take care of most of the other 25 percent of the power needs. However, solar electricity need not be limited to serving this supplementary portion of the nation's requirements, not if an effective method can be found to store it for use anywhere or anytime.

Many scientists think that storing it chemically may be the best method in the long run. Instead of connecting the solar energy to an electric grid system for direct consumption, the energy could be funneled to electrolytic cells designed to generate hydrogen gas, which is a promising substitute for, among other things, gasoline. Thus solar power plants would become fuel-manufacturing facilities rather than on-line central power stations.

A hydrogen-fuel economy of the future would fit in well with solar power. Whenever and wherever the sun shines, solar cells and solar-thermal plants can manufacture hydrogen gas. Where the wind blows and warm ocean currents flow, wind and ocean-thermal-difference plants can also stockpile hydrogen. In the form of hydrogen, energy can be transported and held indefinitely for use as a source of heat and electricity in vehicles, homes, and factories. In a sense, hydrogen would amount to a fossil fuel that is a few days or weeks old instead of eons old. Indeed, with solar power and a hydrogen economy, the need for huge, interconnected power grids across countries like the United States and Canada might well disappear.

Thus the original solar pioneers are now being joined by scores of representatives from the fields of science, government, and industry in the effort to harness the sun to provide cheap and nonpolluting energy. At a time when our dependence on fossil fuels appears to be leading us into a dead end, the development of solar energy is opening new vistas that hold great promise for the future.

Artist's concept of space colonies powered by solar energy. Hinged mirrors along the sides reflect light into interior living spaces. Designed by Gerard K. O'Neill, the colonies would be about sixteen miles long and four in diameter. *NASA*

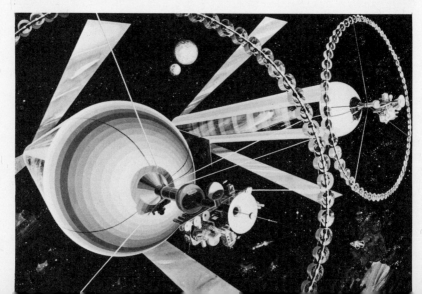

GLOSSARY

array: banks, or rows, of solar-collecting devices mounted together for increased efficiency.

auxiliary heater: conventional heater for use when the sun or stored heat cannot provide sufficient energy for the solar heating system.

bioconversion: process of growing crops specifically for burning to produce power.

biomass: organic material to be converted into power through bioconversion.

central receiver: a solar-thermal power plant, consisting of hundreds of automatically pointed collector mirrors, used to focus sunlight on a central tower.

directional solar collector: solar collectors, usually mirrors, designed to follow the sun to obtain maximum intensity of the sun's rays.

flat-plate collector: a flat plate or plates, usually metal, treated and insulated to absorb sun's heat for use elsewhere.

fossil fuels: fuels, such as coal and oil, which are the remains of animal and plant life that was buried long ago and chemically transformed.

heat reservoir: an insulated tank or container in a solar house, used for temporary storage of a working fluid that has been heated by sunlight.

kilowatt hour: the unit normally used to measure solar energy; the energy expended in 1 hour at the rate of 1 kilowatt (1000 watts).

langley: a unit of solar radiation equivalent to 1 gram calorie per square centimeter of surface upon which sunlight falls.

megawatt: one million watts.

microwave radiation: very short electromagnetic waves; radar.

nuclear reaction: in the sun, the process by which hydrogen atoms are converted into helium atoms, thus releasing tremendous quantities of energy.

ocean-thermal-difference plant: a system constructed to use the differing temperature layers of the ocean to produce energy.

photoelectric cell: a device that produces electric current when light shines upon it; a photocell, or photovoltaic cell. See photovoltaic effect.

photoelectric effect: the effect that produces an electric current when heat is applied to a junction between two metals.

photovoltaic cell: a photoelectric cell. See photovoltaic effect.

photovoltaic effect: production of electric current when light falls upon the junction between certain pairs of dissimilar materials, as differently treated silicon strips.

photovoltaics: term for production of electricity directly from the sun by any combinations or types of voltaic cells.

pyrolysis: chemical change brought about by the action of heat.

radiant energy: see solar energy.

rectifier: device that changes alternating current to direct current.

retrofitting: adapting an existing structure to be heated and/or cooled by solar energy.

Seebeck effect: see photoelectric effect.

solar battery: two or more solar cells connected together to give increased electric current.

solar cell: a photovoltaic cell that uses sunlight as a light source. See photovoltaic cell.

solar constant: the average amount of solar energy normally received at the outer layer of the earth's atmosphere—nearly two calories per square centimeter per minute.

solar cooker: device used to focus the sun's rays for the purpose of cooking food.

solar distillation plant: see solar still.

solar electricity: electricity produced directly from sunlight without the use of solar collectors.

solar energy: radiant energy produced by the sun that reaches the earth. See solar power.

solar-energy collector: a device, usually a mirror, that collects and concentrates the sun's rays for practical uses. See also flat-plate collector.

solar farm: a large area of land upon which arrays of either flat-plate collectors or solar batteries are set up to harvest solar energy for practical use.

solar furnace: a device using large solar mirrors to produce a very high concentration of focused solar radiation.

solar mirror: a curved, highly polished mirror used to focus and concentrate the sun's rays.

solar oven: a device that uses trapped or concentrated sunlight to cook food.

solar power: the rate at which solar energy is produced, usually measured in kilowatt hours. See solar energy.

solar satellite power station: a giant solar-energy-collecting device in orbit around the earth.

solar still: a device that distills fresh water from seawater, or brine, by evaporation and concentration using solar energy.

solar-thermal conversion: any method using the sun's collected and concentrated heat to drive turbines, which in turn generate electricity.

solar water heater: a solar device, usually employing flat-plate collectors, that heats water for domestic purposes.

storage tank: see heat reservoir.

thermoelectric conversion: a method of changing the sun's heat to electric current. See photovoltaic effect.

working fluid: any fluid in a practical solar-energy system that is used as a medium to transfer heat.

INDEX

indicates illustration

126

127